S0-BZL-254

Top 25-sight locator
map (continues on
inside back cover)
◀

Fodor's CITYPACK
london

by Louise Nicholson

Fodor's Travel Publications
New York • Toronto •
London • Sydney • Auckland
www.fodors.com

About This Book

KEY TO SYMBOLS

✚	Map reference to the the accompanying fold-out map, and Top 25 locator map	🚍	Nearest bus route
✉	Address	⛴	Nearest riverboat or ferry stop
☎	Telephone number	♿	Facilities for visitors with disabilities
⏰	Opening/closing times	✋	Admission charge
🍴	Restaurant or café on premises or nearby	↔	Other nearby places of interest
Ⓤ	Nearest subway (underground/tube) station	❓	Tours, lectures, or special events
🚉	Nearest railroad station	➤	Indicates the page where you will find a fuller description
		ℹ	Tourist information

ORGANIZATION

Citypack London is divided into six sections:
- Planning Ahead, Getting There
- Living London—London Now, London Then, Time to Shop, Out and About, Walks, London by Night
- London's Top 25 Sights
- London's Best—best of the rest
- Where to—detailed listings of restaurants, hotels, stores, and nightlife
- Travel facts—packed with practical information

The colors of the tabs on the page corners match the colors of the triangles aligned with the chapter names on the contents page opposite.

MAPS

The fold-out map in the wallet at the back of the book is a comprehensive street plan of London. The first (or only) map reference given for each attraction refers to this map. **The Top 25 locator maps** found on the inside front and back covers of the book itself are for quick reference. They show the Top 25 Sights, described on pages 26–50, which are clearly plotted by number (**1**–**25**, not page number) across the city. The second map reference given for the Top 25 Sights refers to this map.

ADMISSION CHARGES

For attractions we categorize the standard adult rate as follows:
✋ Expensive (over £6), Moderate (£3–£6), and Inexpensive (under £3).

Contents

Planning Ahead

WHEN TO GO

The tourist season is year round, and almost all attractions remain open daily throughout the year. The peak season is between June and September and you should arrive with a hotel reservation and theater tickets. The quietest months are November, January, and February, when you may find discounts on hotel rooms.

TIME

G.M.T. (Greenwich Mean Time) is standard. B.S.T. (British Summer Time) is 1 hour ahead (late Mar–late Oct).

AVERAGE DAILY TEMPERATURE

JAN	FEB	MAR	APR	MAY	JUN	JUL	AUG	SEP	OCT	NOV	DEC
43°F	45°F	50°F	55°F	63°F	68°F	72°F	72°F	66°F	57°F	50°F	45°F

Spring (March to May) has a mixture of sunshine and showers, although winter often encroaches on it.

Summer (June to August) can be unpredictable, with clear skies and searing heat one day followed by sultry grayness and thunderstorms the next.

Fall (September to November) has clear skies that can feel almost summery. Real fall starts in October, and colder weather sets in during November.

Winter (December to February) is generally mild, with the odd cold snap, and snow is rare.

WHAT'S ON

January *Sales*: Shopping bargains at stores all over the city.

February *Chinese New Year*: Dragon dances and fireworks in Soho.

March *Chelsea Antiques Fair*: Chelsea Old Town Hall.

April *Oxford and Cambridge Boat Race* (1st Sat): Putney to Mortlake on the Thames. *London Marathon* (1st Sun): The world's biggest road race.

May *Chelsea Flower Show* (end of May): One of the world's best, at the Royal Hospital, Chelsea.

June *Trooping the Colour* (2nd Sat): The "Colours" (flags) are trooped before the Queen on Horseguards Parade, Whitehall. *Wimbledon* (end of Jun): The world's leading tennis tournament.

July *Promenade Concerts* (Jul–Aug): A series of classical concerts in the Albert Hall.

August *Notting Hill Carnival* (last weekend, Bank Holiday Monday): Europe's biggest.

September *Election of the Lord Mayor of London* (Sep 29): The Lord Mayor and his successor-elect ride in the state coach to the Mansion House.

October *Pearly Kings and Queens* (1st Sun): Service at St. Martin-in-the-Fields.

November *Bonfire Night* (Nov 5): Fires and fireworks commemorate the failed Gunpowder Plot of 1605. *State Opening of Parliament*: Royal procession from Buckingham Palace to the Houses of Parliament.

December *Christmas Tree* (mid-month): Norway's annual gift goes up in Trafalgar Square.

LONDON ONLINE

www.londontouristboard.com
London's official site is up to date and comprehensive with ideas for museums, theater, and restaurants, as well as sections for children, the gay scene, and visitors with disabilities.

www.london-tourist-information.com
A lively website with everything from travel tips to a reservation service, plus useful links to other London-related sites.

www.londontransport.co.uk
London Transport's official site dispenses ideas for what to see and do and ticket information for underground trains and buses. It also has a WAP-enabled journey planner.

www.royal.gov.uk
The official site of the British royal family, with history, royal residences, who's doing what today, and a monthly online magazine.

www.bhrc.co.uk
The British Hotel Reservation Centre website takes bookings, from bed-and-breakfasts to grand hotels. Includes special discounts.

www.londonbb.com
This agency specializes in bed and breakfast accommodations in selected private homes.

www.londonpass.com
On this site you can buy a smart card valid for 1, 2, 3, or 6 days, with unlimited access to 60 top London attractions.

www.hrp.org.uk
London's five great historic palaces, from the Tower of London to Hampton Court.

www.officiallondontheatre.com
The Society of London Theatre's official site, with all the latest theater news plus comprehensive interviews with stars, performance details and theater access for people with disabilities.

PRIME TRAVEL SITES

www.nationaltrust.org.uk
This independent organization looks after 250 buildings in the U.K., including many in the city.

www.english-heritage.org.uk
This government body cares for Britain's historic sites and buildings.

www.fodors.com
A complete travel-planning site. You can research prices and weather; book air tickets, cars, and rooms; ask questions (and get answers) from fellow travelers; and find links to other sites.

CYBERCAFÉS
easyEverything: The international chain started in London is open 24 hours a day, 7 days a week. The 5 cybercafés in London are convenient for tube stations.
✉ 456–459 Strand; Charing Cross/ Embankment stations
✉ 9–16 Tottenham Court Road; Tottenham Court Road station
✉ 358 Oxford Street; Bond Street station ✉ 9–13 Wilton Road; Victoria station
✉ 160–166 Kensington High Street; Kensington High Street station

Getting There

VISAS AND TRAVEL INSURANCE

Passport holders from the U.S., E.U. member countries, and some Commonwealth countries (such as Australia and Canada) do not require a visa. Check your insurance coverage before your trip; if necessary, buy a supplementary travel policy.

ARRIVING

Heathrow and Gatwick are the principal airports serving the city. However, Stansted, Luton, and London City are becoming increasingly busy with traffic from continental Europe. There are train links to Paris and Brussels, and good road links to Channel ports.

40 MILES

Luton Airport ⊠
Bus 1hr 30mins,
£13 return

Stansted Airport ⊠
Bus 1hr 40mins,
£10 return

⊠ **City Airport**
Bus 25–40mins,
£6 single

Heathrow Airport ⊠
Bus 1hr 45mins,
£10 return

⊠ **Gatwick Airport**
Bus 1hr 30mins,
£10 return

MONEY

Try to arrive at the airport with some British coins, or, failing that, a £10 or £5 note. It is highly likely you'll travel to your hotel by tube, as London's subway is known, and large denomination bills are not appreciated.

£5

£10

£20

FROM HEATHROW

Heathrow (☎ 0870 000 0123) has four terminals 15 miles west of central London, all well served by public transportation. On the underground (subway) the Piccadilly line runs from 4:58AM–11:54PM (5:57AM–11:16PM on Sundays), and the trip takes around an hour. The Heathrow Express (☎ 0845 600 1515), a high-speed rail link to Paddington station, runs from 5:10AM–11:40PM. Ticket prices are high for the journey, which takes 20 minutes. Airbus A2 (☎ 08705 747777) routes run 5:40AM–9:53PM but the trip can take more than an hour. Taxis can be picked up outside any terminal; it takes about an hour to make the trip—the time is very dependent on the traffic—and costs around £45.

FROM GATWICK

Gatwick airport (☎ 01293 535353) is 30 miles south of the city center. The Gatwick Express train makes the 30-minute run to Victoria Station every 15 minutes, 24-hours a day. Airbus A5 buses (☎ 08705 747777) run every two hours from 5AM–8:10PM and take around 90 minutes. Taxis cost as much as £90.

FROM STANSTED

Stansted airport (☎ 0870 000 0303) is 35 miles northeast of the city center. The Stansted Skytrain (☎ 0845 484950) runs from 6AM–11:59PM, and takes around 40 minutes. Airbus A6 (☎ 08705 747777) runs from 8AM–10:15PM and takes up to 1 hour 40 minutes. Taxi fares run at around £80.

FROM LUTON AIRPORT

Luton airport (☎ 01582 405100) is 33 miles north of London. There are bus links to Victoria Coach Station, which take around 1 hour 30 minutes and Thameslink trains to King's Cross, which take 40 minutes. Taxis cost about £65.

FROM LONDON CITY AIRPORT

City Airport (☎ 020 7646 0000) has services via the Airport Shuttle Bus to Liverpool Street station every 10 minutes from 6:50AM until 9:10PM Monday to Friday and until 10PM on Saturdays; Sundays from 11AM until 10PM. Taxis wait outside the terminal and cost around £21.

FROM THE CHANNEL TUNNEL

Eurostar (☎ 08705 186186) arrives in Waterloo Station, where you can catch a bus, the underground, or a taxi. Eurotunnel (☎ 08705 353535) is for vehicles only. No reservations are necessary for this service, but fares are lower if you've reserved ahead. They run three times an hour daily between Calais and Folkestone where you can join the M20 to London.

GETTING AROUND

Buses and underground trains run from around 5:30AM to just after midnight, when service is via a night bus. The transportation system is divided into zones—six for the underground and four for buses—and you must have a ticket valid for the zone you are in. If you anticipate more than one journey, buy a travelcard, which allows unlimited use of the underground, buses, and train services in the London area after 9.30AM. Other discounts are available (► 91). Taxis that are available illuminate a yellow "For Hire" sign on top. Hold out your hand to hail them.

DRIVING TIP

Driving in London is slow, parking is expensive, and fines are high—use public transportation. Tickets for the underground (tube) are also valid for use on the buses.

VISITORS WITH DISABILITIES

London is steadily improving its facilities for visitors with disabilities, from stores and theaters to hotels and museums. The Government is introducing free admission for those with disabilities. Newer attractions such as Tate Modern and the London Eye are better equipped than ancient buildings such as Westminster Abbey. Check out the London Tourist Board's comprehensive website www.londontouristboard.com and guidebooks, such as Accessible Britain, covering accommodations (published annually by the English Tourism Council) and The Museum's Guide (published by Artsline).

William Forrester, a lecturer and wheelchair user, leads tailor-made tours in the city (☎ 01483 575401).

Living
London

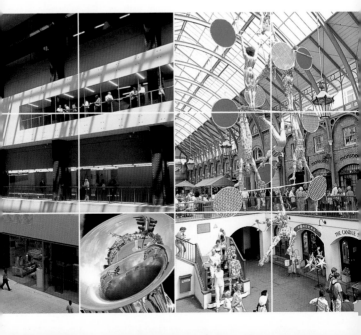

London Now

Above: *you can get a bird's-eye view from the British Airways London Eye*
Right: *from power station to state of the art—Tate Modern*

Few cities celebrated the new millennium with as much verve as London. Known for its pomp, pageantry, and colorful history, the dawn of the year 2000 saw the British capital looking forward rather than back. "New" London ranges from brand-new to dramatically revamped sights, plus trendy restaurants and stores. Whole areas of the capital have been revitalized.

No attractions epitomize today's London better than Tate Modern and the British Airways London Eye. The first is a brilliant example of renovation; the second, a masterpiece of engineering technology. Both captured the public's imagination. Tate Modern, a vast, outdated power station on the depressed south bank of the Thames, was transformed into a vibrant contemporary art gallery. Many of the five million people who toured this museum during the first wildly successful year had never

Above: *café scene in Covent Garden*
Left: *Harley Davidson on the King's Road*

CAFÉ SOCIETY

● Twenty years ago, the idea of sitting at a sidewalk café and sipping a coffee or a beer was considered a "Continental" habit. Londoners ate and drank indoors. Nowadays, however, they think nothing of lingering at outside tables, chatting over an espresso or a cappuchino. In winter, heaters and windbreaks allow the alfresco café society to continue on sunny days. Even that great British invention, the pub, has moved into the open-air. In fine weather, sidewalks can look like obstacle courses; why not sit down and enjoy the passing parade?

LONDON WALKS

● No city has more guided walks. Learn about haunted pubs, Charles Dickens, or the Old Jewish East End. Join a Beatles Magical Mystery Tour; discover saucy Southwark on a Prisons, Pilgrims, Prostitutes, and Players walk. Check listings in *Time Out*; meet the guide at the specified tube station.

11

Above: *diplodocus in the cathedral-like Natural History Museum*
Above right: *the popular Imax Cinema on the South Bank*

entered an art gallery before. What they saw gave them plenty to talk about, even if the sculptures, paintings, and video installations were not always to their taste.

By contrast, the London Eye is pure fun. Dominating the sky above the River Thames, this ultra-modern wheel stands diagonally across from the Big Ben tower. On the slow, smooth glide, even born-and-bred Londoners are amazed by the unexpected views of the capital. Standing at opposite ends of the South

WOULDN'T IT BE LUVERLY

• The chances of meeting a "real" Londoner while on vacation in the capital can be limited. Most city folk are going about their daily business, with little time to sit and chat with strangers. London has long been home to people from around the world. Now, as part of the European Union, you will find French and Italians working in restaurants and cafés, Swedish and Dutch selling clothes in shops, and Belgians and Spanish greeting you at hotel reception desks. You find many Antipodeans in the bars, too. The easiest way to meet a true Londoner is to take one of the famous black cabs. Not only do drivers know their way around the city, they are renowned for their homespun wisdom and outspoken opinions on everything from the royal family to the latest political scandal.

Bank Arts complex, the Eye and Tate Modern have galvanized the long-term regeneration of the south side of the Thames. Here Shakespeare's Globe theater, the BFI IMAX movie theater, and an ever-growing array of bars, restaurants, and arts and crafts galleries are also pulling crowds.

Above: Neal's Yard in Covent Garden—the alternative place for health foods and natural remedies

---

LONDONERS HAVE THEIR SAY

• You won't necessarily find Londoners agreeing. They love to complain about everything from the weather to schools and the National Health Service. While visitors praise the efficiency of the public transportation system, Londoners remember when it was better. After the Greater London Council was abolished in 1983 Londoners had no voice and no authority to whom they could complain. When the new GLA, Greater London Authority, was founded in 1999, Londoners elected their own mayor directly for the first time in their history. The issues faced are the same as other major cities: public transportation, affordable housing, and the environment. With a population of 7.4 million, some 250,000 businesses, and 28 million visitors a year these issues can't be taken lightly.

ON THE BALL

• London has more competitive soccer teams than any other city. Arsenal, Chelsea, West Ham, and Tottenham Hotspur are famous, and weekend tickets are hard to get. Try mid-week, or watch one of the eight other pro clubs. The season runs from August through May.

Above: *inside Canary Wharf*
Right: *carnival time at Notting Hill*
Above right: *cooling off in Trafalgar Square*

TUNE IN

• London's music scene is a magnet for young people, with every sort of rock, pop, and dance style, plus jazz, folk, and world music. Venues include pubs and clubs, and hangar-like temples of electronic sound. And there's always a major Latin American, Asian, or African band in town.

Elsewhere in the capital, the arts have benefited from the completion of major rebuilding projects at the Royal Opera House and Sadler's Wells Theatre. Even more intriguing are two ingenious roofing projects. The first is over the inner courtyard of the British Museum, creating a visitor-friendly Great Court; the second does the same at the Wallace Collection, a fine, small museum near Oxford Street. Somerset House, a grand dame of an 18th-century riverside palace, has had a facelift. Offices were transformed into a museum and a highly reputed restaurant. Where cars once parked choreographed fountains now play, replaced by an ice skating rink in winter.

Beneath the ground, the extension to the Jubilee underground line has proved another success. After years of digging and billions of pounds of investment, this new tube line is an architectural tour de force. Each of the ten stations was individually designed, creating bright clean exciting

new spaces. In addition to providing links between the heart of the city and the South Bank, the rapid and efficient service is helping to regenerate the East End (eastern London).

Not all the millennium projects were so successful. A slim, sculptural new bridge built across the River Thames swayed so alarmingly that it was closed for re-engineering work. Further downstream, the gigantic millennium Dome in Greenwich was universally condemned, and labeled a white elephant. Despite attracting some six million visitors in its opening year, the interior displays were sold off and the building closed. Like all white elephants, its future is unsure.

Overall, however, the effect of new millennium projects has been positive. The buzz and the excitement recalls the 1960s when London led the world in design and creativity. Hand in hand with the new museums and public spaces are cutting-edge restaurants and bars, plus a club scene that is the envy of night owls world-wide. British fashion designers, musicians, architects, and artists are making waves wherever they go: London is hot once again.

SIR CHRISTOPHER WREN

● In the jumble of styles that make up London's cityscape, one architect's legacy dominates. Sir Christopher Wren (1632–1723) designed St. Paul's Cathedral and 51 churches, whose soaring spires inspired builders as far away as the U.S.A. Classics include St. Mary-le-Bow and St. Bride's in Fleet Street.

15

London Then

Above: *the Tower of London from an engraving of 1597*

BEFORE 1000

Emperor Claudius invades Britain in AD 43; a deep-water port, Londinium, is soon established.

In the year 200 the Romans put a wall around Londinium, now capital of Britannia Superior; they withdraw in 410.

THE GREAT FIRE

The fire broke out at a baker's near Pudding Lane on the night of September 2, 1666. Raging for four days and nights, it destroyed four-fifths of the City of London and 13,200 homes. Sir Christopher Wren became the grand architect of the consequent rebuilding of London.

1042 Edward the Confessor becomes king making London capital of England and Westminster his home; begins the abbey church of St. Peter.

1066 The Norman king, William the Conqueror, defeats King Harold at the Battle of Hastings; begins the Tower of London.

1477 William Caxton publishes the first book printed in England.

1485 Tudor rule begins, ending in 1603 with the death of Elizabeth I.

1533 Henry VIII breaks with Rome to marry Anne Boleyn; establishes the Church of England.

1631 Inigo Jones designs London's first square, Covent Garden Piazza.

1649 Charles I is executed in Whitehall; the Commonwealth (1649–53) and Protectorate (1653–59) govern England until Charles II is restored to the throne in 1660.

1666 The Great Fire of London. Sir Christopher Wren begins St. Paul's Cathedral in 1675.

1759 The British Museum, London's first public museum opens.

1837 Queen Victoria begins her reign.

1851 Great Exhibition is held in Hyde Park.

1863 World's first urban underground train service opens. In 1890 the first tube train runs.

1939–45 Blitz bombings destroy a third of the City of London and much of the docks.

1951 Festival of Britain held on the site of the South Bank arts complex.

1960s The Beatles, Carnaby Street, and the King's Road help create "swinging London."

1980s Post-war conservation movements save 30,000 London buildings from demolition.

1981 Revival of Docklands begins.

1994 First Eurostar trains link London and Paris through Channel Tunnel.

2000 Major millennium projects are completed.

2001 Museums in Docklands, Admiralty Arch, Royal Arsenal at Woolwich open; Victoria & Albert Museum's British galleries re-open.

From second left: the Great Fire of London, 1666, from a painting by Lieve Verschuier; the celebrated Festival of Britain, 1951; the "Swinging Sixties" with fashion model Twiggy and friends

GROWING CITY

During the 16th century, London was Europe's fastest-growing city; its population rose from 75,000 to 200,000.

By 1700, London was Europe's biggest and wealthiest city, with about 700,000 people.

London continued to grow, from under 1 million in 1800 to 6.5 million by 1900, peaking in the 1930s and 1940s at 10 million.

The population is now 7 million but rising.

Time to Shop

BEST OF BRITISH

Take home some British souvenirs with a difference. You can buy beautifully crafted umbrellas and walking sticks from James Smith & Sons (✉ 53 New Oxford Street, WC1). For a good British cheese buy a Stilton, all ready and packed, from Paxton & Whitfield (✉ 93 Jermyn Street, SW1). If you want to try some British recipes go to Books for Cooks (✉ 4 Blenheim Crescent, W11) for a large selection of cookbooks. Tea addicts should head for The Tea House (✉ 15A Neale Street, WC2) for a choice of blends and some stylish teapots. English herbs, oils, and toiletries from Culpeper Herbalists (✉ 8 The Market, WC2) make great presents.

If England really is, as Napoleon alleged, a nation of shopkeepers, then London is the head office. There is nothing made anywhere in the world that you cannot find somewhere in the capital. Britain's unique position between Europe and the Americas, bolstered by its colonial connections to Africa, Asia, and Australasia, ensures that saris and spices are as easy to find as Vegemite and rare reggae records. For shoppers, the choice ranges from vibrant street markets to legendary department stores and from off-beat boutiques to smart galleries of paintings and antiques.

It is the range that excites visitors, especially the younger generation. The city is famous for outrageous fashion, bolstered by the annual crop of art, fashion, and design school graduates, all keen to make their mark. Long-established shopping streets, such as Oxford Street and Kensington High Street, offer an enormous choice of competitively-priced clothes and accessories, while markets such as Camden Lock and Portobello Road (see main picture above) are eclectic, ethnic, and inexpensive.

London's souvenirs range from tatty to tasteful. Ever since the Swinging Sixties, anything with a Union Jack flag on it has sold well, from T-shirts to garish hats. By contrast, gifts at the shop in

Something for everyone—shopping in London can be hip or refreshingly traditional. From cobbled markets to Regency arcades—London is the place to shop

Buckingham Palace Mews are more staid: the Queen Victoria range of china, a mini throne for a charm bracelet, or a guardsman puppet. In London Transport's own shop in St. James's Park underground station, the famous map of the tube system appears on mugs, tea towels, and even boxer shorts.

Older shoppers tend to look for traditional clothing, which is more expensive but made to last. Think of men's rugged tweed jackets, flat caps, and handmade shoes. What was once popular with Grandma remains high on many women's lists: delicate fragrances, elegant china, floral printed fabrics, and, of course, cashmere sweaters. They all say "Britain" loud and clear. Despite the proliferation of international chain stores, with their familiar brand names, London still has long-established businesses with worldwide reputations. Visit Burlington Arcade (see main picture above) for its specialist up-market shops in an historic setting. Burberry and Aquascutum are synonymous with raincoats. Harrods has been trading for some 150 years; Selfridges was the country's first department store; and Liberty fabrics are still exotic and luxurious. Their January and July sales are major events on any shoppers' calendar, with visitors from outside the capital and around the world joining Londoners in the hunt for bargains.

TRADITION RULES , OK?

Charles Dickens would recognize some London stores. The Burlington Arcade, off Piccadilly, is a covered walkway with luxury stores and has a liveried beadle to maintain decorum. Other stores display the royal insignia, showing that they supply everything from brushes to jewels to the royal households yet they are open to all (www.royalwarrant.org). John Lobb (✉ 9 St. James's Street, SW1) custom makes shoes and boots for the royal family—and for you, at a price.

Out & About

Above: *the* Cutty Sark *moored at Greenwich.*

INFORMATION

GREENWICH
Distance 4 miles from London Bridge and Tower Hill, 5 miles from Westminster Bridge
Journey time 20 minutes–1 hour
🚈 Docklands Light Railway to Island Gardens, then foot tunnel, or continue to Cutty Sark Station
🚢 Riverboat from Westminster and other piers
🏠 Pepys House, 2 Cutty Sark Gardens, SE10
☎ 020 8858 6376
🕐 Daily 10–5

NATIONAL MARITIME MUSEUM
✉ Romney Road, SE10
☎ 020 8858 4422
🕐 Daily 10–5
🎟 Free

ORGANIZED SIGHTSEEING

A guided tour is a good way to gain in-depth information from a Londoner. Walking tours get into London life. They have good leaders, cost little, and do not require advance reservations. Try the Original London Walks (☎ 020 7624 3978). Bus tours have various pick-up points, including some hotels. Try the Big Bus Company, with live commentary on double-decker buses (☎ 0800 169 1365) or go for a tailor-made tour with a highly trained Blue Badge guide (☎ 020 7495 5504).

EXCURSIONS
GREENWICH

Four miles downstream from the City lies Greenwich. At its core is a favorite royal palace, the Queen's House, designed by Inigo Jones in 1616, which is surrounded by Christopher Wren's buildings for the Royal Naval Hospital. Go early for the whole day. There is plenty to see, plus markets and craft fairs on weekends (➤ 74).

The National Maritime Museum, the world's largest nautical museum, fills the old Royal Hospital School, incorporates Queen's House, and has state of the art galleries opened in 2000. Up the hill is the Royal Observatory, Greenwich—the Greenwich Meridian (0° longitude) passes through here. Nearby, the park's broad terrace provides London's grandest view; behind lie the Ranger's House and the Fan Museum. Also check out the Painted Hall and Chapel inside Wren's Hospital, and two special boats: the *Cutty Sark* built in 1869, and Sir Francis Chichester's yacht *Gipsy Moth IV* in which he undertook his solo round-the-world voyage in 1966–67.

Center: *Hampton Court Palace—fit for a king or queen*
Left: *the regal splendor of Windsor Castle dominates the River Thames*

HAMPTON COURT PALACE

This is London's most impressive royal palace, well worth the journey west out of the city center. When King Henry VIII dismissed Cardinal Wolsey in 1529, he took over his already ostentatious Tudor palace and enlarged it. Successive monarchs altered and repaired both the palace and its 30 acres of Tudor and baroque gardens.

The best way to visit this huge collection of chambers, courtyards, and state apartments is to follow one of the six clearly indicated routes—perhaps Henry VIII's State Apartments or the King's Apartments built for William III, immaculately restored after a devastating fire. Outside, do not miss the Tudor gardens, the Maze, and restored Privy Garden, where there are guided historical walks each afternoon.

WINDSOR

The fairy-tale towers and turrets of Windsor Castle make this official residence of the Queen the ultimate queen's castle. Begun by William the Conqueror, rebuilt in stone by Henry II, it has been embellished periodically. Various parts are open; if the State Apartments and St. George's Chapel are closed, there is still plenty to see. Don't miss Queen Mary's Dolls' House designed by Edward Lutyens. Changing of the Guard is at 11AM.

Outside the castle lie Windsor's pretty, medieval cobblestone lanes, Christopher Wren's Guildhall, and the delightful Theatre Royal. Beyond it, you can explore 4,800-acre Windsor Great Park, cross the Thames to Eton, or visit Legoland.

INFORMATION

HAMPTON COURT
Distance 11 miles
Journey time 30 minutes by train, 3–4 hours by boat
🚇 Waterloo railroad station to Hampton Court
🚤 Riverboat from Westminster Pier

HAMPTON COURT PALACE
✉ East Molesey, Surrey
☎ 020 8781 9500
🕐 Summer: Tue–Sun 9:30–6; Mon 10:15–6. Winter: Tue–Sun 9:30–4:30; Mon 10:15–4:30
💷 Very expensive

WINDSOR
Distance 17 miles
Journey time 35–50 minutes
🚇 Waterloo or Paddington
ℹ 24 High Street
☎ 01753 743900
🕐 Mon–Fri 10–4:30; Sat 10–5; Sun 10–4

WINDSOR CASTLE
☎ 01753 868286
🕐 Mar–Oct: daily 9:45–5. Nov–Feb: daily 9:45–4
💷 Very expensive

Walks

INFORMATION

Distance Approx 1½ miles
Time 2–3 hours,
depending on indoor
visits
Start point ★
Tower Bridge
☩ K6
Ⓒ Tower Hill
End point Royal Festival
Hall, South Bank
☩ G6
Ⓒ Waterloo
Ⓡ Waterloo

THE SOUTH BANK: THE DESIGN MUSEUM TO WESTMINSTER BRIDGE

This walk hugs the bank of the Thames and enjoys superb views across London's core. Begin at Tower Bridge Museum for high-level London views. Then stroll eastwards among the old warehouses and new restaurants of Shad Thames to find Anthony Donaldson's *Waterfall* sculpture in Tower Bridge Piazza, Piers Gough's dramatic *The Circle*, the riverfront Design Museum on Butler's Wharf and the Bramah Tea and Coffee Museum behind.

West of Tower Bridge, the path leads to HMS Belfast and Hay's Galleria for more cafés. The London Dungeon lies behind. Outside the Cottons Centre is a pavilion where a map plots the buildings along the City view. Over London Bridge take in Southwark Cathedral, and a wall and rose window of the l4th-century Winchester Palace's Great Hall.

Between Southwark and Blackfriars bridges are Shakespeare's Globe theatre, Tate Modern and the Oxo Tower. The riverfront widens at the South Bank arts complex; the London Aquarium lies beyond. Take Hungerford footbridge for Charing Cross, Westminster Bridge for Westminster.

0   ½ km
0   ½ mile

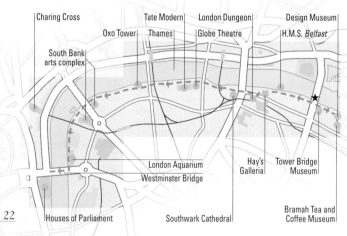

Charing Cross | Tate Modern | London Dungeon | Design Museum
Oxo Tower | Thames | Globe Theatre | H.M.S. *Belfast*
South Bank arts complex

London Aquarium | Hay's Galleria | Tower Bridge Museum
Westminster Bridge

Houses of Parliament | Southwark Cathedral | Bramah Tea and Coffee Museum

THE TWO CITIES: CITY OF WESTMINSTER TO THE CITY OF LONDON

The heart of Westminster is still Westminster Abbey and the Houses of Parliament—there is a good view of the riverfront from the south end of Westminster Bridge.

From statue-filled Parliament Square, Whitehall leads up past Downing Street, Horse Guards, and Banqueting House, to Trafalgar Square, home of the National Gallery. The National Portrait Gallery is at the end of St. Martin's Lane. Farther on, past the Coliseum, turn right through New Row into Covent Garden, a good place to stop for refreshment. On the piazza, find the London Transport Museum and nearby, the Theatre Museum. Down on the Strand, turn left and go through Aldwych to the Courtauld Gallery.

In Fleet Street, winged dragons mark the boundary of the City of London and Westminster. Just before Chancery Lane, an alley on the right leads to Temple Church and the Inner and Middle Inns. Farther on, Johnson's Court (between Nos. 166 and 167), leads to Dr. Johnson's House. St. Paul's Cathedral stands at the top of Ludgate Hill. Behind it, Watling Street leads to Bow Lane and a choice of restaurants.

INFORMATION

Distance 2–2½ miles
Time 3–6 hours, depending on museum and church visits
Start point ★
Westminster Bridge
🚇 G6
🚇 Westminster
End point Bow Street
🚇 G5
🚇 Mansion House

London by Night

Above: *if the weather permits join the sidewalk party in Soho*
Above right: *theaterland— Shaftesbury Avenue*

WALK THE WALK

The mile-long stretch of riverside between Westminster and London bridges bustles by night, as well as by day. The London Eye (open until 10:30PM in summer) is magical after dark. On the opposite bank, illuminated landmarks include the Houses of Parliament and Somerset House. At Oxo Tower Wharf, go to the top floor for a drink or a meal. There are few better views of London. Admire Tate Modern (open until 10PM Fridays and Saturdays) and the Globe. Rest your feet at a riverside pub.

London changes with the seasons, especially after dark. In the depths of winter, dusk falls at 4:30 in the afternoon; in summer it stays light until 10PM. The fogs that added atmosphere to Alfred Hitchcock's films are long gone, but winters can be damp, so Londoners walk with energy and purpose, rather than at a leisurely pace. Perhaps this explains the popularity of the "pub crawl," which includes stops every few minutes to go indoors and warm up. Guided after-dark walks to historic and haunted pubs are an ideal way to explore the city in fall and winter.

Come summer, London's outdoors comes into its own. Londoners enjoy the sound of music at concerts in such grand settings as Hampton Court, Kenwood, Hyde Park, and Kew Gardens. The music ranges from classical and opera to jazz and rock 'n' roll. In elegant Kensington, the Holland Park Theatre puts on first-class opera and ballet against a backdrop of the remains of the 17th-century Holland House. The Regent's Park Open Air Theatre has mounted fine performances of Shakespeare for over 70 years. Some venues provide covered seating; elsewhere spectators sit on the grass. Although all venues have small restaurants, most Londoners arrive with food and wine and have a picnic. It's part of the pleasure of summer in the city.

Year round the diversity of the club scene is legendary and with many changing themes weekly, check before you go. There are tried and tested venues for older clubbers and a host of new wave options (► 84) pulsing in the city.

LONDON's
top 25 sights

The sights are shown on the maps on the inside front cover and inside back cover, numbered **1**–**25** across the city

THE
NATURAL
HISTORY
MUSEUM

Top Visitor Attraction
Holiday Which Magazine

Children and Senior Citizens Free

Royal Botanical Gardens, Kew

HIGHLIGHTS

- Arriving by riverboat
- Japanese Gateway and Pagoda
- Gallery walks, Palm House
- Temperate House
- Springtime woods and dells
- Oak Avenue to Queen Charlotte's Cottage

INFORMATION

- ✚ Off fold-out map; Locator map off A3
- ✉ Kew Road, Kew, Richmond
- ☎ 020 8940 1171
- 🕐 Daily from 9:30AM. Closing time varies.
- 🍴 Good
- Ⓠ Kew Garden
- 🚉 Kew Bridge
- ♿ Excellent ▣ Moderate
- ❓ Guided tours 11, 2 from Victoria Gate; orchid show Feb–Mar

The Princess of Wales Conservatory

Whether the trees are shrouded in winter mists, the azaleas are bursting with blossoms, or the lawns are dotted with summer picnickers reading Sunday newspapers, Kew Gardens never fail to work their magic.

Royal beginnings The 300-acre gardens, containing 44,000 different plants and many glorious greenhouses, make up the world's foremost botanical research center. But it began modestly. George III's mother, Princess Augusta, planted 9 acres around tiny Kew Palace in 1759, helped by gardener William Aiton and botanist Lord Bute. Architect Sir William Chambers built the Pagoda, Orangery, Ruined Arch, and three temples. Later, George III enlarged the gardens to their present size and Sir Joseph Banks (head gardener 1772–1819), who had traveled with Captain Cook, planted them with specimens from all over the world.

Victorian order When the gardens were given to the nation in 1841, Sir William Hooker became director for 24 years. He founded the Department of Economic Botany, the museums, the Herbarium, and the Library, while W. A. Nesfield laid out the lake, pond, and the four great vistas: Pagoda Vista, Broad Walk, Holly Walk, and Cedar Vista.

The greenhouses Chambers' Orangery is now a shop and restaurant. Decimus Burton designed the Palm House (1844–48) and Temperate House (1860–62, when it was the world's largest greenhouse), which preserves some plants that are extinct in their countries of origin. See too Waterlily House (1852) and the Princess of Wales Conservatory (1987). The exhibition, Evolution, tells the story of plants down the centuries.

Kensington Palace & Gardens

It gives King William III a human dimension that he suffered from asthma, a modern complaint, and so moved out of dank Whitehall Palace to a mansion in the clean air of tiny Kensington village.

The perfect location The year he became king, 1689, William and his wife Mary bought their mansion, perfectly positioned for London socializing and country living. They brought in Sir Christopher Wren and Nicholas Hawksmoor to remodel and enlarge the house, and moved in for Christmas.

A favorite royal home Despite the small rooms, George I introduced palatial grandeur with Colen Campbell's staircase and state rooms, elegantly decorated by William Kent. Meanwhile, Queen Anne added the Orangery (the architect was Nicholas Hawksmoor, the woodcarver Grinling Gibbons) and annexed a chunk of royal Hyde Park, a trick repeated by George II's wife, Queen Caroline, who created the Round Pond and Long Water to complete the 275-acre Kensington Gardens. Today, a wide variety of trees are the backdrop for sculptures (George Frampton's fairytale Peter Pan), monuments (Prince Albert), and contemporary exhibitions at the Serpentine Gallery.

A very special childhood On May 24, 1819, Queen Victoria was born here. She was baptized in the splendid Cupola Room, spent her childhood in rooms overlooking the gardens (now filled with Victoria memorabilia) and, on June 20, 1837, learned here she was to be queen. Later she opened her childhood home to the public. A permanent exhibition about Diana, Princess of Wales, opened in 2001.

HIGHLIGHTS

- King's Grand Staircase
- Presence Chamber
- Wind dial in the King's Gallery
- King's Drawing Room
- Princess Victoria's dolls' house
- Round Pond
- Tea in the Orangery
- Walks
- Diana, Princess of Wales Exhibition
- Italian Gardens

INFORMATION

- C6; Locator map off A3
- Kensington Gardens, W8
- 020 7937 9561
- Daily 10–6; Nov–Feb 10–5
- Café in palace (winter) or Orangery (summer)
- High Street Kensington or Queensway
- Few
- Expensive; family tickets
- Natural History Museum (➤ 28), Science Museum (➤ 29), V&A Museum (➤ 30)
- Guided tour every 30 minutes

Natural History Museum

HIGHLIGHTS

- Cromwell Road facade
- Giant gold nugget
- Fossilized frogs
- Afghan lapis lazuli
- How the memory works
- Restless Surface Gallery
- Marine Invertebrate Gallery

INFORMATION

- C7; Locator map A3
- Cromwell Road, SW7; also entrance on Exhibition Road
- 020 7942 5000
- Mon–Sat 10–5:50; Sun 11–5:50
- Meals, snacks, picnic areas
- South Kensington
- Excellent
- Free
- Kensington Palace (➤ 27), Science Museum (➤ 29), V&A Museum (➤ 30)
- Regular tours, lectures, films, workshops

Top: the entrance hall
Below: the East Wing

Before you go in, look at the museum building. It looks like a Romanesque cathedral and is wittily decorated with a zoo of animals to match its contents: extant animals on the west side, extinct ones on the east side.

Two museums in one Overflowing the British Museum where they were originally housed, the Life Galleries were moved to Alfred Waterhouse's honey-and-blue-striped building in 1880. They tell the story of life on earth. The story of the earth itself is told in the Earth Galleries, beginning with a 300-million-year-old fossil of a fern. The Darwin Centre, (opens 2002), uses IT to make most of the museum's 70 million objects and the work of its 300 or so scientists accessible worldwide.

Dinosaurs in the Life Galleries The nave of Waterhouse's cathedral contains a plaster cast of the vast skeleton of the 150-million-year-old diplodocus (the original is in Pittsburgh). Lively exhibition galleries focus on the relevance of the dinosaur world, the human body, mammals, birds, the marine world today, and "creepy crawlies" (the 800,000 known species of insect are added to every year)—all with plenty of slides, models, and hands-on games.

The Earth Galleries These offer a fascinating exploration of our planet. The Earthquake Experience is set in a Japanese supermarket, the Restless Surface explores the effects of natural forces on the earth, and the Earth's Treasury looks at the gemstones and minerals lying beneath the earth's crust.

Science Museum

Even if you are no scientist, it's thrilling to understand how a plane flies, how Newton's reflecting telescope worked, or how we receive satellite television. You'll find answers using hands-on interactives. This is science made fun.

Industry and science Opened in 1857 and once part of the Victoria & Albert Museum, this is the museum that comes closest to fulfilling Prince Albert's educational aims when he founded the South Kensington Museums after the Great Exhibition of 1851. Its full title is the National Museum of Science and Industry. Therefore, over the five floors, which contain more than 60 collections, the story of human industry, discovery, and invention is recounted through various tools and products, from exquisite Georgian cabinets to a satellite launcher.

Science made fun People of all ages walk, talk, laugh, and get excited by what they see here. You can see how vital every day objects were invented and then developed for use. The spinning wheel, steam engine, car, and television have changed our lives. The industrial society in which we live could not do without plastic, but how is it made?

All kinds of science The galleries vary from rooms of beautiful 18th-century objects to in-depth explanations of abstract concepts: you can use the hands-on equipment in Flight Lab to learn the basic principles of flying. The Wellcome Museum of the History of Medicine, on the topmost floors, includes an exhibit on pre-historic bone surgery and an X-ray room. The interactive Challenge of Materials and the high-tech Wellcome Wing explore science, technology, and the complex world we know today.

HIGHLIGHTS

- Demonstrations
- Taking part in Launch Pad
- The hands-on basement area
- Flight Lab
- Apollo 10 module
- Puffing Billy
- Amy Johnson's airplane, *Jason*
- 18th-century watches and clocks
- The Wellcome Wing
- Historical characters explaining their achievements

INFORMATION

- ✚ C7; Locator map A3
- ✉ Exhibition Road, SW7
- ☎ 0870 870 4868
- 🕐 Daily 10–6
- 🍴 Cafés, picnic area
- Ⓢ South Kensington
- ♿ Excellent, plus helpline
  ☎ 020 7942 4446
- 🎟 Free
- ❓ Guided tours, demonstrations, historic characters, lectures, films, workshops
- ↔ Natural History Museum (► 28)

Top: Apollo 10 module in the Exploration of Space Gallery

29

Victoria & Albert Museum

HIGHLIGHTS

- Medieval ivory carvings
- Jones porcelain collection
- Glass Gallery
- Shah Jahan's Jade Cup
- Canning Jewel
- New Raphael Gallery
- Frank Lloyd Wright Room
- British Galleries
- The Hereford Screen

INFORMATION

- ✚ D7; Locator map A3
- ✉ Cromwell Road, SW7
- ☎ 020 7942 2000
- 🕐 Daily 10–4:45; Wed and last Fri of month 10–10
- 🍴 Basement restaurant, café
- 🚇 South Kensington
- ♿ Very good
- 🎫 Free
- ↔ Natural History Museum (► 28), Science Museum (► 29)
- ❓ Guided tours, talks, courses, concerts

Detail, facade

Part of the Victoria & Albert Museum's glory is that each room is unexpected; it may contain a French boudoir, plaster casts of classical sculptures, or exquisite contemporary glass, diverting you so happily that sometimes you will never reach your original goal.

An optimistic foundation The V&A, as it is fondly known, started as the South Kensington Museum. It was Prince Albert's vision: arts and science objects available to all people to inspire them to invent and create, with the accent on commercial design and craftsmanship. Since it opened in 1857, its collection has become so encyclopedic and international that today, it is the world's largest decorative arts museum.

Bigger and bigger Its size is unmanageable: 145 galleries cover 7 miles of gallery space on six floors. Its content is even more so: barely 5 percent of the 44,000 objects in the Indian department can be on show. Larger museum objects include whole London house facades, grand rooms, and the Raphael Cartoons. Despite this, contemporary work has always been energetically bought: more than 60 percent of furniture entering the museum is 20th century.

Riches and rags Not every object in the V&A is precious: there are everyday things, unique pieces, and opportunities to discover a fascination for a new subject—perhaps lace, ironwork, tiles, or Japanese textiles. The best way to tackle the V&A is either to select a favorite piece and go headlong for it, or wander happily for an hour or so, feasting on any objects that catch your eye. See the lavishly refurbished British Galleries, reopened in Nov 2001; and Daniel Libeskind's controversial Spiral project may yet be realized.

Kenwood House & Hampstead Heath

For many north Londoners, sunny Sunday mornings on Hampstead Heath are an essential part of life: locals walk their dogs and babies, sit reading the newspapers, enjoy the fine London views, or drop into Kenwood House to see a Rembrandt or two.

Kenwood House When in 1754 William Murray, Earl of Mansfield and George III's Chief Justice, bought his country house outside pretty Hampstead village spa, he brought in London's most fashionable architect, Robert Adam, to remodel it, and employed Humphry Repton to landscape the gardens. A later owner, Edward Guinness, Earl of Iveagh, hung the walls with Rembrandts, Gainsboroughs, Vermeers, and Romneys before giving the whole package, the Iveagh Bequest, to the nation.

The people's heath When Victorian London was expanding, it was the people of Hampstead who saved their valuable, open heathland from the developers' claws. Since 1829 they have preserved, piece by piece, a total of 825 acres of rolling woodland, open grass, and spectacular views—the walled Hill Garden was added only in 1960. It is "to be kept forever...open, unenclosed and unbuilt on."

A place of many moods The heath is full of action and color when weekend kite-flyers meet on Parliament Hill. It is a place for sports, perhaps swimming or boating in Hampstead Ponds, playing hockey on East Heath, enjoying a game of tennis, or simply taking a quiet walk. There are arts celebrations, too, the best of which are the summer lakeside concerts that Londoners listen to as they picnic on the sloping lawns in front of Kenwood House.

HIGHLIGHTS

- Azaleas in the Hill Garden
- Library in Kenwood House
- Lakeside concerts
- London view from beside Kenwood House
- Oak, beech, and sweet chestnut woods
- Parliament Hill
- Crossing the Heath from Hampstead to Highgate
- Rembrandt's *Portrait of the Artist* in Kenwood House
- Carpets of spring daffodils around Kenwood

INFORMATION

- ✚ Off fold-out map; Locator map off A1
- ✉ Kenwood House, Hampstead Lane, NW3
- ☎ 020 8348 1286
- 🕐 Kenwood House Apr–Sep: daily 10–6. Oct: daily 10–5. Nov–Mar: daily 10–4. The Heath daily 8AM–dusk
- 🍴 Restaurant, café
- Ⓜ Kenwood House: Golders Green. The Heath: Hampstead, Belsize Park, Highgate, or Kentish Town
- 🚌 Kenwood House: 210, 271. Parliament Hill: 214, C2, C11, C12
- 🚉 Gospel Oak, Hampstead Heath
- ♿ Good 🅵 Free
- ❓ Guided tours for groups, outdoor concerts

31

Regent's Park

Regent's Park has all an urban explorer could wish for: big open spaces, a lake to row on, spectacular gardens, ducks and swans in quantity, ideal picnic spots, theater and music, and free peeks at the elephants in the zoo.

The Prince's plan Regent's Park is the result of a remarkable coincidence of royal enlightenment, architectural theater, peaceful times, and a large tract of land becoming available. In 1811 the Prince Regent, later George IV, and his architect, John Nash, conceived and completed a Regency backbone for London stretching from St. James's Park up Regent Street and Portland Place to Regent's Park. After vast earth-moving activities, the park was given its undulating lawns, lake, garden, and trees, all ringed by grand row house backdrops and dotted with just eight of the 56 planned villas.

From the nobles to the people What was designed as a garden city for nobles is now the most elegant of London parks. It has been open to the public since 1835, when Regent's Canal was one of the busiest stretches of canal in Britain. Londoners flocked to visit the zoo, Inner Circle (later Queen Mary's) Gardens, and Avenue Gardens, which W. A. Nesfield designed in 1864. Its 487 acres easily absorb Muslims strolling from the gold-domed Central Mosque, patrons of the Open Air Theatre, cricketers—and many others besides.

The canal at Little Venice

HIGHLIGHTS

- Queen Mary's Gardens
- Lakeside strolls
- Lolling on deckchairs by the bandstand
- Wildfowl Breeding Centre
- Boating on the lake
- Nesfield's restored Avenue Gardens
- Canal boat trip from the zoo to Little Venice
- 98 species of duck
- Picnicking on the lake's north bank
- Summer barbecues at the open-air theater

INFORMATION

- E3; Locator map B1
- Marylebone Road, NW1
- 020 7486 7905
- Daily 7AM to shortly before dusk (times are posted on information boards at each gate)
- Restaurant, cafés
- Baker Street, Regent's Park, Great Portland Street, or Camden Town
- Very good
- London Zoo (➤ 33), Madame Tussaud's waxworks & Planetarium (➤ 61)
- Information boards at entrances include plans; boats for rent on the lake and children's boating pond; summer weekend bandstand music; open-air theater and musicals May–Sep

London Zoo

When you visit the zoo, have a look at the gentle Asian elephants—first from Regent's Park, then inside the zoo—having a bath, throwing dust over their backs, eating, lazing about, and playing with their keeper.

Exotic animals for Londoners In 1826 Sir Stamford Raffles, who established Singapore Colony, founded the Zoological Society of London with Sir Humphry Davy. Four years later it opened 5 acres of its gardens to the public, and met with immediate success. The Society's own collection of exotic animals—zebras, monkeys, kangaroos, and bears—was soon enlarged by the royal menagerie from Windsor Castle and the royal zoo from the Tower of London.

Extraordinary animals Over the years new arrivals have included Tommy the chimpanzee in 1835 and, in 1836, the giraffes, which set a trend for giraffe-patterned fabric. Jumbo and Alice, the African elephants, were also exceedingly popular with visitors. Meanwhile, the world's first reptile house, aquarium, and insect houses were constructed.

A modern zoo Aware of the worldwide controversy over zoos, London Zoo is maintaining its place at the forefront of animal conservation and education. It houses the Institute of Zoology, which carries out research, and funds important ground-breaking fieldwork. The Children's Zoo has a "petting paddock" and a center to teach children how to care for pets. While deer roam, lions roar, and birds screech, there are talks, demonstrations, and the Web of Life conservation center to encourage awareness of the earth's fragility.

HIGHLIGHTS

- Asian elephants
- Big cats
- Children's Zoo Pet Care Centre
- Lord Snowdon's aviaries
- Reversed lighting to see nocturnal mammals
- Feeding time for lions
- Cavorting chimpanzees
- Web of Life center
- Baby rhinos

INFORMATION

- ✚ E2 (for entrance); Locator map B1
- ✉ Regent's Park, NW1
- ☎ 020 7722 3333
- 🕐 Daily 10–5:30
- 🍴 Restaurant, cafés, and kiosks
- Ⓒ Camden Town
- Ⓔ Camden Town
- ♿ Good
- 💷 Very expensive
- ↻ Regent's Park (► 32)
- ❓ Lectures, talks, workshops, regular animal feeding times; animal action programs daily; animal adoption schemes

Top: the elephant enclosure

Buckingham Palace

HIGHLIGHTS

- Liveried beadles in the Queen's Gallery
- Changing of the Guard
- State Coach, Royal Mews
- Nash's facade, Quadrangle
- Gobelin tapestries in the Guard Room
- Throne Room
- Van Dyck's portrait of Charles I and family
- Table of Grand Commanders, Blue Drawing Room
- Secret royal door in the White Drawing Room
- Garden Shop

INFORMATION

- F6; Locator map C3
- The Mall, SW1
- 020 7799 2331
- Queen's Gallery: 020 7799 2331 for opening times.
  Royal Mews Apr–Oct: Mon–Thu noon–3:30. Oct–Dec: Mon, Wed noon–4. Closed Ascot week and ceremonial occasions.
  State Rooms, Buckingham Palace Aug–Sep: daily 9:30–4:30. Last admission at 4:30.
- Victoria, St. James's Park, or Green Park
- Victoria
- Excellent
- Very expensive
- No photography

Of the London houses now open to visitors, the Queen's own home must be the most fascinating of all: where else can you see a living sovereign's private art, drawing rooms, and horse harnesses?

Yet another palace The British sovereigns have moved around London quite a bit over the years; from Westminster to Whitehall to Kensington and St. James's, and finally to Buckingham Palace. It was George III who in 1762 bought the prime-site mansion, Buckingham House, as a gift for his new bride, the 17-year-old Queen Charlotte, leaving St. James's Palace to be the official royal residence.

Grand improvements When the Prince Regent finally became King George IV in 1820, he and his architect, John Nash, made extravagant changes using honey-colored Bath stone, all to be covered up by Edward Blore's facade added for Queen Victoria. Today, the 600 rooms and 40-acre garden include the State Apartments, offices for the Royal Household, a movie theater, swimming pool, and the Queen's private rooms overlooking Green Park.

Queen Elizabeth II opens her home The Queen inherited the world's finest private art collection. The Queen's Gallery (reopening in spring 2002) exhibits some of her riches. In the Royal Mews, John Nash's stables house gleaming fairytale coaches, harnesses, and other apparel for royal ceremonies. Make sure you do not miss the Buckingham Palace Summer Opening, when visitors can wander through the grand State Rooms, resplendent with gold, pictures, porcelain, tapestries, and of course, thrones.

St. James's Park

Even if you drop in to St. James's Park merely to eat a sandwich and laze on a deck chair while listening to the band's music, you can usually spot a trio of palaces across the duck-filled lake and over the tips of the weeping willows.

Royal through and through St. James's Park is the oldest and most thoroughly royal of London's nine royal parks, surrounded by the Palace of Westminster, St. James's Palace, Buckingham Palace, and the remains of Whitehall Palace. Kings and their courtiers have been frolicking here since Henry VIII laid out a deer park in 1532 and built a hunting lodge that became St. James's Palace. James I began the menagerie, which included pelicans, crocodiles, and an elephant who drank a gallon of wine daily.

French order Charles II, influenced by Versailles, near Paris, redesigned the park to include a canal (where he swam), Birdcage Walk (where he kept his aviaries), and the graveled Mall, where he played pell mell, a courtly French game similar to croquet. Then George IV, helped by John Nash and influenced by Humphry Repton, softened the garden's formal French lines into the English style, making this 93-acre park of blossoming shrubs and undulating, curving paths a favorite with all romantics.

Nature dominates As the park is an important migration point and breeding area for birds, two full-time ornithologists look after up to 1,000 birds from more than 45 species. Among the fig, plane, and willow trees, seek out the pelicans living on Duck Island, a tradition begun when the Russian Ambassador gave some to Charles II.

HIGHLIGHTS

- Springtime daffodils
- Whitehall from the lake bridge
- Feeding the pelicans, 3PM
- Views to Buckingham Palace
- Duck Island in springtime
- The fact that it is still not enclosed

INFORMATION

- ✚ F6; Locator map C3
- ✉ The Mall, SW1
- ☎ 020 7930 1793
- 🕐 Daily dawn to midnight
- 🍴 Restaurant, café
- Ⓢ St. James's Park, Green Park, or Westminster
- 🚉 Victoria
- ♿ Very good
- 🎫 Free
- ↔ Buckingham Palace (➤ 34), Banqueting House (➤ 39)
- ❓ Changing the Guard (contact tourist information). Occasional bird talks; summer bandstand music

The Whitehall skyline seen from the park

Tate Britain

Moving through the galleries past Gainsborough portraits, Turner landscapes, and Hepworth sculptures, this is an intimate social history of Britain told by its painters.

Two for one The Tate Gallery was opened in 1897, named after the sugar millionaire Henry Tate, who paid for the core building and donated his Victorian pictures to put inside it. Until 2000, the national collections of British and international modern art were housed there, with increasingly inadequate space. Then, the international modern collection went to Bankside Power Station and was renamed Tate Modern (► 47). The national collection now fills Henry Tate's refurbished building, completed in October 2001, which is renamed Tate Britain.

British art Recognizing that many people are unfamiliar with British art, the galleries are helpfully divided into four chronological suites. You can follow the visual story of British art from 1500 until today. Although paintings, sculptures, installations, and works in other media will be changed regularly, you may well see Nicholas Hilliard's icon-like portrait of Elizabeth I, Van Dyck's lavish court portraits, and richly colored Pre-Raphaelite canvases. Do not miss the great Turner collection housed in the adjoining Clore Gallery.

The Turner Prize Britain's most prestigious and controversial prize to celebrate young British talent is run by the Tate and awarded each fall following an exhibition of nominees' works. Founded in 1984, winners have included Damien Hurst and Chris Ofili, while Gilbert and George, Tracey Emin, Sam Taylor-Wood, and Tony Cragg have all been nominees.

Westminster Abbey

The very best time to be in the abbey is for the 8AM service, sometimes held in tiny St. Faith's Chapel, followed by a wander in the silent nave and cloisters before the crowds arrive.

The kernel of London's second city It was Edward the Confessor who in the 11th century began the rebuilding of the modest Benedictine abbey church of St. Peter which was consecrated in 1065. The first sovereign to be crowned there was William the Conqueror, on Christmas Day 1066. Successive kings were patrons, as were the pilgrims who flocked to the Confessor's shrine. Henry III (1216–72) employed Master Henry de Reyns to re-begin the Gothic abbey that stands today, and Henry VII (1485–1509) built his Tudor chapel with its delicate fan vaulting. Since William I, all sovereigns have been crowned here—even after Henry VIII broke with Rome in 1533 and made himself head of the Church of England; and all were buried here up to George II (after which Windsor became the royal burial place ► 21).

The West Front

Daunting riches The abbey is massive, full of monuments, and very popular. From the nave's west end enjoy the view and Master Henry's achievement, then look over the Victorian Gothic choir screen into Henry V's chantry. Having explored the chapels, the royal necropolis, and Poets' Corner, leave time for the quiet cloisters.

HIGHLIGHTS

- Portrait of Richard II
- Sir Isaac Newton memorial
- Sir James Thornhill's window
- Henry VII's Chapel
- Edward the Confessor's Chapel
- St. Faith's Chapel
- Tile floor, Chapter House
- Little Cloister and College Garden
- Weekday sung evensong (except Wed) at 5PM

INFORMATION

- ✚ G7; Locator map D3
- ✉ Broad Sanctuary, SW1; entry by North Door
- ☎ 020 7222 7110; services 020 7222 5152
- 🕐 Nave and Royal chapels Mon–Fri 9:30–3:45; Sat 9:30–1:45. Photography Wed 6PM–7PM. Chapter House, Pyx Chamber, Abbey Museum, and College Garden daily various hours. Closed before special services, Sun, Dec 24–25, Good Fri, and Commonwealth Observance Day.
- 🍴 Café in cloisters
- Ⓦ Westminster
- 🚇 Victoria
- 🅶 Good
- 🎫 Services free. Royal Chapels moderate
- ❓ Guided tours

Houses of Parliament

INFORMATION

Big Ben is for many the symbol of London: they love its tower, its huge clear clockface, and its thundering hour bell. Summer tours of the whole building reveal its beauty, intriguing traditions, and government workings.

Powerhouse for Crown and State William the Conqueror made Westminster his seat of rule to watch over the London merchants (he also built the Tower of London ➤ 50). It was soon the center of government for England, then Britain, then a globe-encircling empire. It was also the principal home of the monarchs until Henry VIII moved to Whitehall.

Mother of parliaments Here the foundations of Parliament were laid according to Edward I's Model Parliament of 1295; a combination of elected citizens, lords, and clergy. This developed into the House of Commons (elected Members of Parliament) and the House of Lords (unelected senior members of State and Church). Henry VIII's Reformation Parliament of 1529–36 ended Church domination of Parliament and made the Commons more powerful than the Lords.

A building fit for an empire Having survived the Catholic conspiracy to blow up Parliament (on November 5, 1605, Guy Fawkes' night), almost all the buildings were destroyed by a fire in 1834. Kingdom and empire needed a new headquarters. With Charles Barry's plans and A. W. Pugin's detailed design, a masterpiece of Victorian Gothic was created. Behind the river facade decorated with statues of rulers, the Lords is on the left and the Commons on the right. If Parliament is in session, there is a flag on Victoria Tower or, at night, a light on Big Ben.

Banqueting House

It is chilling to imagine Charles I calmly walking across the park from St. James's Palace to be beheaded outside the glorious hall built by his father. The magnificent ceiling was painted for Charles by Peter Paul Rubens.

London's most magnificent room This, all that remains of Whitehall Palace, was London's first building to be coated in smooth, white Portland stone. Designed by Inigo Jones and built between 1619 and 1622, it marked the beginning of James I's dream to replace the original sprawling Tudor palace with a 2,000-room Palladian masterpiece. In fact, it was only the banqueting hall that was built. Inside, the King hosted small parties in the crypt and presided over lavish court ceremonies upstairs.

The Rubens ceiling The stunning ceiling was commissioned by James's son, Charles I. Painted between 1634 and 1636 by Peter Paul Rubens, the leading baroque artist based in Antwerp, the panels celebrate James I, who was also James VI of Scotland. Nine allegorical paintings show the unification of Scotland and England and the joyous benefits of wise rule. Rubens was paid £3,000 and given a knighthood for the work.

The demise of Whitehall Palace This palace has brought a fair share of bad luck to its occupants. Cardinal Thomas Wolsey lived so ostentatiously that he fell from Henry VIII's favor. Henry moved in, making it his and his successors' main London royal residence. It was here that Charles I was beheaded on January 30, 1649, and William III suffered from the dank river air. A fire in 1698 wiped out the Tudor building, leaving only the stone Banqueting House.

HIGHLIGHTS

- Sculpted head of Charles I
- Weathercock put on the roof by James II
- Rubens ceiling
- Allegory of James I between Peace and Plenty
- Allegory of the birth and coronation of Charles I
- Lunchtime concerts
- Whitehall river terrace in Embankment Gardens
- The video and self-guiding audio tour

INFORMATION

- G6; Locator map D3
- Whitehall, SW1
- 020 7930 4179
- Mon–Sat 10–5. Last admission 4:30. Closed Dec 24–Jan 1, public hols, and for functions
- Westminster, Charing Cross, or Embankment
- None
- Moderate
- Occasional lunchtime concerts

Inigo Jones's facade

National Portrait Gallery

HIGHLIGHTS

- *Self-portrait with Barbara Hepworth,* Ben Nicholson
- Icon-like *Richard II*
- The Tudor Galleries
- *Samuel Pepys,* John Hayl
- *Queen Victoria,* Sir George Hayter
- *The Brontë Sisters,* Branwell Brontë
- *Isambard Kingdom Brunel,* John Callcott
- *Florence Nightingale,* William White
- *Sir Peter Hall,* Tom Phillips
- Using the self-guiding audio tour

INFORMATION

- ✚ G5; Locator map C2
- ✉ St. Martin's Place, WC2
- ☎ 020 7306 0055
- 🕐 Daily 10–6; Thu, Fri until 9PM. Closed Good Fri
- 🍴 Café, rooftop restaurant
- Ⓜ Leicester Square or Charing Cross
- 🚊 Charing Cross
- ♿ Good
- 💷 Free except for special exhibitions
- ↔ National Gallery (➤ 41)
- ❓ Lectures, events

It is always fascinating to see what someone famous looks like and how they chose to be painted—for instance, you would never expect Francis Drake to be in red courtier's, rather than sailor's, clothes.

A British record Founded in 1856 to collect portraits of the great and good in British life, and so inspire others to greatness, this now huge collection is the world's most comprehensive of its kind. There are oil paintings, watercolors, caricatures, silhouettes, and photographs.

Start at the top The galleries, incorporating a new wing (2000), are arranged in chronological order, starting on the top floor—reached by stairs or elevator. Henry VIII kicks off a visual Who's Who of British history that moves through inventors, merchants, engineers, explorers, and empire builders to modern politicians, always accompanied by their observers, the writers. Here you'll find Isambard K. Brunel, Robert Clive and Warren Hastings of India, Winston Churchill, and Margaret Thatcher. There is Chaucer in his floppy hat, Kipling at his desk, and A. A. Milne with Christopher Robin and Winnie-the-Pooh on his knee. Lesser-known sitters also merit a close look, such as the 18th-century portrait of the extensive Sharp Family, who formed an orchestra and played at Fulham every Sunday.

A modern record, too At first, the Victorians insisted upon entry only after death, but this rule has been broken. Among the many contemporary portraits, you may find those of the football star David Beckham, Beatle Sir Paul McCartney, actors John Hurt and Stephen Fry, painter Patrick Heron, and Joan Collins.

National Gallery

Here is a collection of tip-top pictures— and for free, so you can drop in for a few minutes' peace in front of Leonardo da Vinci's cartoon in the Sainsbury Wing or Rubens's ravishing *Samson and Delilah*.

A quality collection   Founded in 1824 with just 38 pictures, the National Gallery now has about 2,000 paintings, all on show. Spread throughout William Wilkins's neoclassical building and the Sainsbury Wing extension (opened 1991), they provide an uncramped, extremely high-quality, concise panorama of European painting from Giotto to Cézanne. Most modern and British pictures are at the Tate Galleries (➤ 36, 47).

Free from the start   Unusually for a national painting collection, the nucleus is not royal but the collection of John Julius Angerstein, a self-made financier. From the start it was open to all, including children, free of charge, and provided a wide spectrum of British painting within a European context—aims that are still maintained. Arrivals for the millennium included Cimabue's *Virgin and Child Enthroned with Angels* and Henry Raeburn's *The Archers*.

A first visit   To take advantage of the rich artistic panorama, why not choose a room from each of the four chronologically arranged sections? Early paintings by Duccio di Buoninsegna, Jan van Eyck, Piero della Francesca, and others fill the Sainsbury Wing. The West Wing has 16th-century pictures, including Michelangelo's *Entombment*, while the North Wing is devoted to 17th-century artists such as Van Dyck, Rubens, Rembrandt, Velàzquez, and painters of the Dutch school. Finally, the East Wing runs from Chardin through Gainsborough to Matisse and Picasso.

HIGHLIGHTS

- *Virgin Enthroned*, Cenni di Peppi Cimabue
- Cartoon, Leonardo da Vinci
- *Pope Julius II*, Raphael
- *The Arnolfini Wedding*, Van Eyck
- Equestrian portrait of Charles I by Van Dyck
- *The Triumph of Pan*, Poussin
- *Arabian Stallion*, George Stubbs
- *The Archers*, Henry Raeburn
- *The House of Cards*, Jean-Baptiste-Siméon Chardin
- *Mr and Mrs William Hallett*, Gainsborough
- *La Pointe de Hève*, Monet
- View from Wilkins's entrance

INFORMATION

- ✚ G6; Locator map C2
- ✉ Trafalgar Square, WC2
- ☎ 020 7839 3321
- 🕐 Mon, Tue, Thu–Sun 10–6; Wed 10–9. Late openings for some special exhibitions. Closed Good Fri
- 🍴 Brasserie, basement café
- Ⓔ Charing Cross or Leicester Square
- 🚉 Charing Cross
- ♿ Excellent
- 🎟 Free except for special exhibitions
- ❓ Guided tours, lectures, films, picture opinon service

Covent Garden Piazza

HIGHLIGHTS

- Bedford arms and motto over the Market entrances
- St. Paul's Covent Garden
- 1920s and 1930s underground posters
- Craft stands in Apple Market
- The Royal Opera House
- Jubilee Hall Market
- How the underground works, London Transport Museum
- Charles H. Fox's make-up shop, Tavistock Street
- Neal Street, nearby

INFORMATION

- ✚ G5; Locator map D2
- ✉ Covent Garden Piazza, WC2
- 🍴 Plentiful, all prices
- Ⓒ Covent Garden
- 🚆 Charing Cross
- ♿ Good
- 🎫 Free except museums
- ↔ National Portrait Gallery (► 40), Somerset House (► 43), British Museum (► 45)

London Transport Museum

- ✉ 39 Wellington Street, WC2
- ☎ 020 7379 6344
- 🕐 Mon–Thu, Sat, Sun 10–6; Fri 11–6. Last admission 5:15. Closed Dec 24–26
- 🍴 Café
- ♿ Very good
- 🎫 Moderate
- ❓ Weekend guided tours, lectures, films, workshops

It is always enjoyable to cut through the piazza, to see clowns cavorting in front of St. Paul's Church, a busker cheering on the vendors, and people meeting up to enjoy the city.

London's first square Charles I was against expanding beyond the City but Francis Russell, the Earl of Bedford, owned a prime piece of land just west of it. Around 1630, the Earl paid the King £2,000 for a building license and used Inigo Jones to lay out London's first residential square. An instant success, it became a distinctive London feature.

Covent Garden When society left, the vegetable market moved in, together with taverns, gambling dens, and prostitutes. Charles Fowler's Central Market (1831) brought order, as did Floral, Flower, and Jubilee Halls, making this London's central fruit and vegetable

A Punch and Judy show

market until 1974. Locals saved the area from demolition, and today the restored halls and rebuilt Royal Opera House complex (► 56) make the piazza sparkle again.

London Transport Museum This tells the story of the world's largest urban public transportation system, which covers more than 500,000 miles. There are buttons to push and plenty of vehicles. Star attractions include the underground simulator, the touch screens in six languages, actors on the vehicles—and the shop.

Somerset House

Transformed from a lavish but forgotten building into a riverside palace, spend a day here moving from French Impressionist masterpieces to English silver to some of Russia's finest art.

A palatial home   A majestic, triple-arched gateway leads from the Strand into Sir William Chamber's English Palladian government offices (1776–86). Within the gateway, the Courtauld Collection is housed in rooms lavishly decorated for the Royal Academy, before its move to Piccadilly. Ahead, the great courtyard has fountains, a theater, an ice-rink, and café tables, according to the season. The rooms overlooking the Thames, accessed from the courtyard or from the Embankment, contain a restaurant, café, and two special interest treats: the Gilbert Collection and the Hermitage Rooms.

The Courtauld Gallery   A stunning collection of French Impressionist paintings collected by the industrialist Samuel Courtauld—Manet, Renoir, Cezanne, Van Gogh, Gaugin—inspired five other collectors to donate art. So the art feast also has Italian Renaissance panels, Rubens canvases, and Ben Nicolsons.

The Gilbert Collection   Arthur Gilbert, born in London, made his fortune in California and spent it on art in three fields: Roman and Florentine mosaics, gold and silverware, and 18th-century gold snuff boxes. Then he gave it all to his home town.

The Hermitage Rooms   An outpost of the State Hermitage Museum in St. Petersburg, the 500 or so exhibits selected from its astoundingly rich collection change regularly, so you really need to drop in to see what's new on each visit.

HIGHLIGHTS

Courtauld Collection:
- *La Lodge*, Renoir
- *Bar at the Folies-Bergere*, Manet
- A roomful of Rubens paintings
- *The Trinity*, Botticelli

Gilbert Collection:
- Micro-mosaic table top with views of Rome
- Silver ewer, Paul de Lamerie
- 18th-century enamel snuff boxes

INFORMATION

- ✚ G5; Locator map D2
- ✉ Somerset House, Strand, WC2
- ☎ Courtauld: 020 7848 2526; Gilbert: 020 7420 4080; Hermitage: 020 7845 4630. To book a timed entry ticket 020 7413 3398
- 🕐 Courtauld: Mon–Sat 10–6; Sun 2–6. Gilbert: daily 10–6. Hermitage: Mon–Sat 10–6, Sun 12–6
- 🍴 Cafés, restaurant
- Ⓜ Temple
- 🚉 Blackfriars, Charing Cross
- ♿ Excellent
- 💲 Moderate
- ⟷ Covent Garden Piazza (► 42), Sir John Soane's Musuem (► 44), Dr. Johnson's House (► 54)
- ❓ Full time education program

43

Sir John Soane's Museum

HIGHLIGHTS

- *The Rake's Progress, The Election*, Hogarth
- Sarcophagus of Seti I
- Lawrence's portrait of Soane
- Monk's Parlor
- Works by Turner, Canaletto
- Model Room

INFORMATION

- ✚ G5; Locator map D2
- ✉ 13 Lincoln's Inn Fields, WC2
- ☎ 020 7405 2107
- ◷ Tue–Sat 10–5. 1st Tue of the month 6PM–9PM. Closed Dec 24–26, Jan 1, Good Fri
- Ⓗ Holborn
- Ⓡ Farringdon
- Ⓤ Free
- ⇔ Somerset House (▶ 43), British Museum (▶ 45), Dickens House (▶ 54)
- ？ Guided tours Sat 2:30

As you move about the gloriously over-furnished rooms of Soane's two houses and into the calm upstairs drawing room, his presence is so strong you feel you would not be surprised if he were there to greet you.

Soane the architect This double treasure-house in leafy Lincoln's Inn Fields, central London's largest square, is where the neoclassical architect Sir John Soane lived. First he designed No. 12 and lived there from 1792. Then he bought No. 13 next door, rebuilt it with cunningly proportioned rooms, and lived there from 1813 until his death in 1837. Meanwhile, he also designed Holy Trinity church on Marylebone Road (1824–48), and parts of the Treasury, Whitehall. His model for his masterpiece, the (destroyed) Bank of England, is here (re-created rooms now form the bank's museum ▶ 52). No. 14 opens as a center for Adam Studies in 2004.

Soane the collector Soane was an avid collector. He found that every art object could inspire his work, so his rooms were a visual reference library. Hogarth's paintings unfold from the walls in layers. There are so many sculptures, paintings, and antiquities that unless you keep your eyes peeled you will miss a Watteau drawing, a Greek vase, or something better.

The ghost of Soane Sir John's ingenious designs pervade every room, as do the stories of his passion for collecting. For example, when an Egyptian sarcophagus arrived, he gave a three-day party in its honor.

Behind the facade a labyrinth of rooms houses a bizarre collection

British Museum

It's fun to choose your own seven wonders of the world in the British Museum. It's likely the bronzes from the Indian Chola dynasty and the lion-filled reliefs that once lined an Assyrian palace will be on the list.

The physician founder Sir Hans Sloane, after whom Sloane Square is named, was a fashionable London physician, "interested in the whole of human knowledge" and an avid collector of everything from plants to prints. When he died in 1753 aged 92 he left his collection of more than 80,000 objects to the nation on condition that it was given a permanent home. Thus began the British Museum, opened in 1759 in a 17th-century mansion, Britain's first public museum and now its largest, covering 13½ acres.

It grew and it grew To Sloane's collection were added many others. Kings George II, III, and IV made magnificent gifts, as did other monarchs. These, with the Townley and Elgin Marbles, burst the building's seams and the architect Robert Smirke designed a grand new museum, completed by his son, Sydney, in 1857. Even so, because the booty from expeditions and excavations poured in continuously, the Natural History collections went to South Kensington (➤ 28). With the departure of the British Library (➤ 56) to St. Pancras in 1998, the central Great Court has been redeveloped and the Sainsbury Galleries built for the African collections.

Coming to grips with the British Museum A good way to explore "that old curiosity shop in Great Russell Street" is to pick up a plan in the Great Court, see what special events are on, choose at the most three rooms to see, and set off to find them. For peace and quiet, go early.

HIGHLIGHTS

- Oriental antiquities
- Sainsbury Galleries
- Rosetta Stone
- Current prints and drawings
- Islamic Art
- Mildenhall and Sutton Hoo treasures
- Elgin Marbles
- Assyrian and Egyptian rooms
- Roman Britain Gallery
- Norman Foster's Great Court redevelopment

INFORMATION

- ✚ G4; Locator map D2
- ✉ Great Russell Street, WC1 (another entrance in Montague Place)
- ☎ 020 7636 1555
- 🕐 Sat–Wed 10–5:30; Thur, Fri 10–8:30. Great Court: Mon–Wed 9–9; Thu–Sat 9AM–11PM; Sun 9–6.
- 🍴 Restaurant, cafés
- Ⓔ Holborn or Tottenham Court Road
- ♿ Very good
- 💷 Free except for some temporary exhibitions, tours, and late openings
- Ⓒ Covent Garden Piazza (➤ 42), Percival David Foundation of Chinese Art (➤ 53)
- ❓ Full educational program

St. Paul's Cathedral

HIGHLIGHTS

- Sung evensong
- Frescoes and mosaics
- Wren's Great Model in the riforium (upstairs)
- Triple-layered dome weighing 76,000 tons
- Jean Tijou's sanctuary gates
- Wellington's memorial
- *Light of the World*, Holman Hunt
- The great climb
- Wren's epitaph under the dome

INFORMATION

- J5; Locator map E2
- St. Paul's Churchyard, EC4
- 020 7236 4128
- Mon–Sat 8:30–4:30, last admission 4. Galleries 9:30–4.30, last admission 3:30. Services include Mon–Sat 5; Sun 11, 3:15
- Refectory in the crypt
- St. Paul's or Mansion House
- City Thameslink or Cannon Street
- Very good
- Moderate
- Museum of London (► 49), Bank of England Museum (► 52), Dr. Johnson's House (► 54), St. Margaret, Lothbury (► 57)
- Guided tours; organ recitals; masses in Jul

To sneak into St. Paul's for afternoon evensong, and sit gazing up at the mosaics as the choir's voices soar, is to savor a moment of absolute peace and beauty. Go early or late to avoid the crowds.

Wren's London After the restoration of the monarchy in 1660, artistic patronage bloomed under Charles II. Then, when the Great Fire of London destroyed four-fifths of the City in 1666, Christopher Wren took center stage, being appointed King's Surveyor-General in 1669, aged just 37. The spires, towers, and steeples of his 51 new churches (23 still stand) surrounded his masterpiece, St. Paul's.

The fifth St. Paul's This cathedral church for the diocese of London was founded in AD 604 by King Ethelbert of Kent. The first four churches burned down. Wren's, built in stone and paid for with a special coal tax, was the first English cathedral built by a single architect, the only one with a dome, and the only one in the English baroque style. The funerals of Admiral Lord Nelson, the Duke of Wellington, and Sir Winston Churchill were held here; statues and memorials of Britain's famous crowd the interior and crypt.

The great climb The 530 steps to the top are worth the effort. Shallow steps rise to the Whispering Gallery for good views of Sir James Thornhill's dome frescoes and the 19th-century mosaics. The external Stone Gallery has telescopes and benches; above is the Golden Gallery.

Tate Modern

The national collection of modern art fills the magnificent spaces of George Gilbert Scott's monumental Bankside Power Station by the Thames, making it London's most radical new focus for the new millennium.

World Class Art On a par with the Metropolitan Museum of Modern Art in New York in its range, richness, and quality, the collection that once shared space with the British Collection (► 36) now blossoms in its own huge spaces. Swiss architects Herzog & de Meuron have created an exciting contemporary structure within the handsome brick building, making it ideal for exhibiting large-scale works of art in an innovative way. Gallery events, cafés, a big shop, and a rooftop restaurant complete the total package for a great day out and a focal point for the now rejuvenated South Bank.

20th century and more Works exhibited here continue the story of art begun by the National Gallery. The most influential artists of the 20th century are all represented, including Picasso, Matisse, Dali, Duchamp, Rodin, Gabo, and Warhol—as well as British artists such as Bacon, Hodgkin, Hockney, and Caro. Works on display change regularly, and there are special exhibitions. But together they represent all the major periods and movements of the 20th century, from Surrealism to Conceptual Art.

Daringly contemporary Tate Modern is itself a modern building in an old skin. It connects to the north bank via the Millennium Bridge. It augments its collection with the cutting edge of contemporary art, and even its display methods are new. Four suites of rooms, each devoted to one subject, mix together pieces from various periods.

HIGHLIGHTS

Although displays change look out for works by:
● Pablo Picasso
● Claude Monet
● Henri Matisse
● Constantin Brancusi
● Jackson Pollock
● Mark Rothko
● Bridget Riley
● Marcel Duchamp
● Andy Warhol
● Richard Hamilton
● David Hockney

INFORMATION

✚ J6; Locator map E2
✉ Bankside, SE1
☎ 020 7887 8008
🕐 Sun–Thu 10–6; Fri, Sat 10–10
🍴 Cafés, restaurant
Ⓜ Blackfriars or Southwark
Ⓡ Blackfriars or London Bridge
♿ Very good
💷 Free, charge for some special exhibitions
↔ Shakespeare's Globe (► 22), St. Paul's Cathedral (► 46), The Tower of London (► 50), Southwark Cathedral (► 22, 57), London Eye (► 60)
❓ Full educational program. Free daily guided tours of the four suites of rooms—landscape, still life, the nude, and history—are available.

47

St. Bartholomew-the-Great

HIGHLIGHTS

- Rahere's tomb
- William Bolton's window
- Medieval font
- Tudor tomb of Sir Walter Mildmay
- Ramsden church silver
- Any choral service
- Alfredo Roldan's altarpiece
- Sung evensong

INFORMATION

- ✚ J4; Locator map E2
- ✉ West Smithfield, EC1
- ☎ 020 7606 5171
- 🕐 Tue–Fri 8:30–5 (winter: 8:30–4); Sat 10:30–1:30; Sun 2–6.
  Sun services 9AM, 11AM (choral), 6:30PM (choral)
- Ⓜ Barbican, Farringdon, or St. Paul's
- 🚆 Farringdon
- ♿ Good
- 💷 Free (donation encouraged)
- ↔ St. Paul's Cathedral (➤ 46), Museum of London (➤ 49)
- ❓ Exceptional choir

A Sunday evening spent at St. Bartholomew's is truly memorable: while trucks arrive at Smithfield's meat market, you can answer the ringing bells and pass under the great stone arch into a hidden, medieval world.

A court jester for founder Henry I's court jester, Rahere, became an Augustinian canon. While on pilgrimage to Rome he was cured of malaria, had a vision of St. Bartholomew, and took a vow. On his return, the King gave him land to found St. Bartholomew's Hospital and Priory—London's first hospital but one of four monasteries in the area.

London's oldest church Rahere's priory church, built in 1123, is London's oldest surviving church, the City's only 12th-century monastic church, and its best surviving piece of large-scale Romanesque architecture. The remains (the nave and cloisters are gone) give an idea of the magnificence of London's dozen or so medieval monastic churches.

Entering a different world The church lies through a 13th-century stone arch topped by a Tudor gatehouse, which once led into the great priory church's west end. Today, a path runs the length of what was the ten-bay nave down to the present west door. Here is the choir, the ambulatory, and the Lady Chapel (built by Rahere), whose roofs are supported by honey-colored walls and sturdy, circular columns. The minimal decoration makes the impact all the more powerful. Two tombs sit uneasily together here: those of the founder, Rahere (*d*1143; tomb 1404), and of the destroyer, Richard Rich, who bought the building from Henry VIII after the dissolution of the monasteries.

Museum of London

A visit here is easily the best way to cruise through London's 2,000 years of history, pausing to see a Roman shoe, the Lord Mayor's State Coach, or an old shop counter; and it is even built on the West Gate of London's Roman fort.

A museum for London This is the world's largest and most comprehensive city museum, opened in 1976 in a building by Powell and Moya. The collection combines the old Guildhall Museum's City antiquities with the London Museum's costumes and other culturally related objects. Plenty of building work and redevelopment in the City of London since the 1980s, allied with increased awareness about conservation, has ensured a steady flow of archeological finds into the collection.

A museum about London The story of London is long and can be confusing. The building is, appropriately, in the barbican of the Roman fort, and the rooms are laid out chronologically to keep the story clear. Starting with prehistoric (a new London Before gallery opens in 2002) and Roman times (do not miss the peep-hole window down to 2nd-century barbican remains), the rooms work through the medieval, Tudor, and Stuart periods. A highlight here is the re-enactment of the Great Fire of London in 1666. The Georgian, Victorian, and 20th-century rooms mix low life with high—from Newgate Gaol to Spitalfields silks, and ending with the World City Gallery, plus lively comtemporary exhibitions.

A museum about Londoners People make a city, so in every room it is Londoners who are really telling the story, whether it is through their Roman storage jars, their Tudor leather clothes, or their Suffragette posters.

HIGHLIGHTS

- Pre-history gallery
- Hoard of 43 gold Roman coins
- Sptialfields woman (Roman)
- Viking grave
- Fragments from the Eleanor Cross
- Tudor jewelry
- Model of Tudor London
- Pepys's chess set
- 17th-century paneled room
- World City Gallery

INFORMATION

- ✚ J4; Locator map E2
- ✉ 150 London Wall, EC2
- ☎ 020 7600 3699
- 🕐 Mon–Sat 10–5:50; Sun noon–5:50. Closed Dec 24–26, Jan 1
- 🍴 Restaurant, café
- Ⓑ Barbican, Moorgate, or St. Paul's
- Ⓡ Moorgate, Farringdon, Liverpool Street, or City Thameslink
- ♿ Excellent
- 🎫 Free
- ↔ St. Paul's Cathedral (► 46), St. Bartholomew-the-Great (► 48), Barbican (► 80–81)
- ❓ Full education program

Mural depicting a scene from the Great Fire

H.M. The Tower of London

The restored rooms of Edward I's 13th-century palace bring the Tower alive as the royal palace and place of pageantry it was; for some, they are more interesting than the Crown Jewels.

HIGHLIGHTS

- Medieval Palace
- Raleigh's room
- Imperial State Crown
- Tower ravens
- Grand Punch Bowl, 1829
- St. John's Chapel

INFORMATION

- K5; Locator map F2
- London, EC3
- 020 7709 0765
- Mar–Oct: Mon–Sat 9–5; Sun 10–5. Nov–Feb: Tue–Sat 9–4; Sun, Mon 10–4
- Cafés
- Tower Hill
- Fenchurch Street, Cannon Street, or London Bridge
- Excellent for Jewel House
- Very expensive
- Design Museum (➤ 52), H.M.S. *Belfast* (➤ 60), Tower Bridge Experience (➤ 59)
- Tours every 30 minutes

A "Beefeater"

Medieval fortress The Tower of London is Britain's best medieval fortress. William the Conqueror (1066–87) began it as a show of brute force, and Edward I (1272–1307) completed it. William's Caen stone White Tower, built within old Roman walls, was an excellent defense: it was 90 feet high, with walls 15 feet thick, and space for soldiers, servants, and nobles. Henry III began the Inner Wall, the moat, the watergate—and the royal zoo. Edward I completed the Inner Wall, built the Outer Wall, several towers, and Traitor's Gate, and moved the mint and Crown Jewels here from Westminster.

Scenes of splendor and horror Stephen (1135–54) was the first king to live here, James I (1603–25) the last. From here Edward I went in procession to his coronation and Henry VIII paraded through the city bedecked in cloth of gold. Here the Barons seized the Tower to force King John to put his seal to the Magna Carta in 1215; and here two princes were murdered while their uncle was being crowned Richard III. Since 1485 it has been guarded by Yeoman Warders or "Beefeaters".

Seven centuries of history The Tower has been palace, fortress, state prison, and execution site. There is much to see. Come early and see the Crown Jewels and the Crowns and Diamonds Exhibition, then take a break along the Wharf.

LONDON's
best

London's Best

Museums & Galleries

DULWICH PICTURE GALLERY

Dulwich Picture Gallery's magnificent core collection of 400 paintings was assembled for the King of Poland's projected national gallery. When the king abdicated, the collection was offered unsuccessfully to Britain for the same purpose. The art dealer who put it together, Noel Desenfans, gave it to Sir Francis Bourgeois, who donated it to Dulwich College. Housed in a building designed by Sir John Soane, and opened in 1814, it was England's first public art gallery.

The Edwardian Room, in the Geffrye Museum

BANK OF ENGLAND MUSEUM

See how Britain's monetary system and banking ideas have grown since 1694.

➕ J5 ✉ Bartholomew Lane, EC2 ☎ 020 7601 5545 🕐 Mon–Fri 10–5 🚇 Bank 💷 Free

CABINET WAR ROOMS

The underground headquarters for Sir Winston Churchill's War Cabinet during World War II.

➕ G6 ✉ Clive Steps, King Charles Street, SW1 ☎ 020 7930 6961 🕐 Oct–Mar: daily 10–6. Apr–Sep: daily 9:30–6 🚇 St. James's Park or Westminster 💷 Moderate

DESIGN MUSEUM

Founded by design guru Sir Terence Conran to stimulate design awareness. Good shop.

➕ L6 ✉ Butler's Wharf, Shad Thames, SE1 ☎ 020 7403 6933 🕐 Mon–Fri 11:30–6; Sat, Sun 10:30–6 🍴 Café, restaurant 🚇 Tower Hill or London Bridge 🚉 London Bridge 💷 Moderate

DULWICH PICTURE GALLERY

European art. (See panel).

➕ Off map at K10 ✉ College Road, SE21 ☎ 020 8693 5254 🕐 Tue–Fri 10–5; Sat, Sun 11–5 🍴 Restaurant 🚉 North or West Dulwich 💷 Moderate. Free on Fri

GEFFRYE MUSEUM

Almshouses furnished in period style, 1550 until the present day.

➕ K3 ✉ Kingsland Road, E2 ☎ 020 7739 9893 🕐 Tue–Sat 10–5; Sun, public hols 2–5PM. Closed Good Fri 🍴 Café 🚇 Old Street, bus 243; Liverpool Street, bus 149, 242 💷 Free

HOUSE MUSEUMS (► 54)

IMPERIAL WAR MUSEUM
Focuses on the social impact of 20th-century warfare through film, painting, and sound archives. The Holocaust Museum is not suitable for children.
➕ H7 ✉ Lambeth Road, SE1 ☎ 020 7416 5000 🕐 Daily 10–6 🍴 Restaurant, café Ⓜ Lambeth North, Elephant & Castle, or Waterloo 🚇 Waterloo 💲 Free

JEWISH MUSEUM
One of two museums devoted to London's Jewish community (the other is in Finchley). See also Imperial War museum above.
➕ F3 ✉ 129–131 Albert Streert, NW1 ☎ 020 7284 1997 🕐 Mon–Thu 10–4; Sun 10–5 Ⓜ Camden Town 💲 Moderate

LONDON AQUARIUM
An aquatic spectacular. Follow the story of a stream, an ocean, a coral reef, and more.
➕ G6 ✉ County Hall, Riverside Building, Westminster Bridge Road, SE1 ☎ 020 7967 8000 🕐 Daily 10–6. Last admission 5PM 🍴 Café Ⓜ Westminster 💲 Expensive

MUSEUM IN DOCKLANDS
Opened in 2001, a host of objects and displays tell the story of London's river, port, and people from Roman times until the present day.
➕ Off map from N5 ✉ Warehouses Nos. 1 &2, West India Quay, Canary Wharf, E14 ☎ 020 7515 1162 🕐 Phone for opening times Ⓜ West India Quay 💲 Moderate

PERCIVAL DAVID FOUNDATION OF CHINESE ART
Sublime Chinese ceramics.
➕ G4 ✉ 53 Gordon Square, WC1 ☎ 020 7387 3909 🕐 Mon–Fri 10:30–5 Ⓜ Russell Square 💲 Free

PHOTOGRAPHERS' GALLERY
Contemporary photos in the heart of London.
➕ G5 ✉ 5–8 Great Newport Street, WC2 ☎ 020 7831 1772 🕐 Mon–Sat 11–6; Sun 12–6 Ⓜ Leicester Square 💲 Free

ROYAL ACADEMY
Major art shows, plus the annual Summer Exhibition. Don't miss rooftop Sackler Galleries.
➕ F6 ✉ Burlington House, Piccadilly, W1 ☎ 020 7300 8000 🕐 Sat–Thu 10–6; Fri 10–8:30 🍴 Restaurant, café Ⓜ Green Park or Piccadilly 💲 Expensive

WALLACE COLLECTION
Artworks in an 18th-century town house. See panel.
➕ E5 ✉ Hertford House, Manchester Square, W1 ☎ 020 7935 0687 🕐 Mon–Sat 10–5; Sun noon–5 🍴 All day courtyard café/restaurant Ⓜ Bond Street 💲 Free

WHITECHAPEL ART GALLERY
The hub of vibrant East End art activities.
➕ L5 ✉ 80 Whitechapel High Street, E1 ☎ 020 7522 7888 🕐 Tue, Thu–Sun 11–5; Wed 11–8 🍴 Café Ⓜ Aldgate East 💲 Free

The Pacific Tank at the London Aquarium

THE WALLACE COLLECTION

The Wallace Collection is the product of five generations of discerning art collectors. The 1st Marquess of Hertford bought Ramsays and Canalettos; the 2nd acquired Gainsborough's *Mrs Robinson*; the 3rd preferred Sèvres and Dutch 17th-century pictures; and the 4th, in Paris during the Revolution, snapped up quality French art. His illegitimate son, Sir Richard Wallace, added his own Italian majolica, Renaissance armor, bronzes, and gold.

53

House Museums

Dr. Johnson's House

APSLEY HOUSE (WELLINGTON MUSEUM)

Splendid mansion built for Arthur Wellesley, Duke of Wellington (1759–1852).

➕ E6 ✉ Hyde Park Corner, SW1 ☎ 020 7499 5676 🕐 Tue–Sun 11–5 🚇 Hyde Park Corner 💷 Moderate

CARLYLE'S HOUSE

Thomas Carlyle, Scottish philosopher and historian, lived here from 1834 until his death in 1881.

➕ D8 ✉ 24 Cheyne Row, SW3 ☎ 020 7352 7087 🕐 Apr–Oct: Wed–Sun, public hols 11–5 🚇 Sloane Square 💷 Moderate

CHISWICK HOUSE

Lord Burlington's exquisite country villa (1725–29), whose formal garden is an integral part of his design. Don't miss a stroll along nearby Chiswick Mall.

➕ Off map at A8 ✉ Burlington Lane, W4 ☎ 020 8995 0508 🕐 Apr–Sep: daily 10–6. Oct: daily 10–5. Nov–Mar: Wed–Sun 10–4 🍴 Café 🚇 Turnham Green 🚉 Chiswick 💷 Moderate

DICKENS HOUSE

The great novelist lived here 1837–39, while he completed *Pickwick Papers*, wrote *Oliver Twist* and *Nicholas Nickleby*, and began *Barnaby Rudge*.

➕ H4 ✉ 48 Doughty Street, WC1 ☎ 020 7405 2127 🕐 Mon–Sat 10–5 🚇 Russell Square, Chancery Lane, or King's Cross 🚉 King's Cross 💷 Moderate

DR. JOHNSON'S HOUSE

Dr. Samuel Johnson lived here between 1749 and 1759 while compiling his dictionary.

➕ H5 ✉ 17 Gough Square, EC4 ☎ 020 7353 3745 🕐 May–Sep: Mon–Sat 11–5:30. Oct–Apr: 11–5 🚇 Chancery Lane or Blackfriars 🚉 Blackfriars 💷 Moderate

HAM HOUSE

Thameside baroque mansion dating from 1610; house and garden meticulously restored.

➕ Off map at A10 ✉ Ham, Richmond, Surrey ☎ 020 8940 1950 🕐 House Apr–Oct: Sat–Wed 1–5. Closed Nov–Mar. Gardens Sat–Wed 10:30–6 (or dusk) 🍴 Restaurant 🚇 Richmond, then bus 371 💷 Moderate

LEIGHTON HOUSE

Lord Leighton made his reputation when Queen Victoria bought one of his paintings. George Aitchison then designed his home-cum-studio (1861–6). The fashionable painter and esthete gave the rooms rich red walls edged with ebonized wood. Their centerpiece is the Arab Hall, one of London's most exotic rooms, lined with Persian and Saracenic blue and green tiles collected by Leighton during his travels.

LEIGHTON HOUSE (see panel)

➕ B7 ✉ 12 Holland Park Road, W14 ☎ 020 7602 3316 🕐 Wed–Mon 10–5:30 🚇 High Street Kensington 💷 Free

Statues & Monuments

BURGHERS OF CALAIS
Auguste Rodin's muscular bronze citizens (1915).
✚ G7 ✉ Victoria Tower Gardens, SW1 🚇 Westminster

CHARLES I
This superb equestrian statue of Charles I was made by Hubert Le Sueur in 1633.
✚ G6 ✉ South side of Trafalgar Square 🚇 Charing Cross
🚃 Charing Cross

DUKE OF WELLINGTON
The only London hero to have three equestrian statues: the others are in St. Paul's Cathedral and outside the Duke's home, Apsley House (➤ 54).
✚ J5 ✉ Opposite the Bank of England, EC2 🚇 Bank

EROS
Alfred Gilbert's memorial (1893) to the philanthropic 7th Earl of Shaftesbury (1801–85) actually portrays the Angel of Christian Charity, not Eros.
✚ F5 ✉ Piccadilly Circus, W1 🚇 Piccadilly Circus

MONUMENT
Wren's 202-foot Doric column commemorates the Great Fire (1666). Worth climbing the dark corkscrew of 311 steps for the view.
✚ K5 ✉ Monument Street, EC3 🚇 Monument

NELSON'S COLUMN
Horatio, Viscount Nelson (1758–1805) went up on to his 172-foot column in 1843; the hero died as he defeated the French and Spanish at Trafalgar.
✚ G6 ✉ Trafalgar Square 🚇 Charing Cross 🚃 Charing Cross

OLIVER CROMWELL
King-like Cromwell, Lord Protector of England from 1653 to 1658, looks across Parliament Square.
✚ G7 ✉ Houses of Parliament 🚇 Westminster

PETER PAN
George Frampton's statue (1912) of J. M. Barrie's creation, the boy who never grew up.
✚ C6 ✉ Long Water, Kensington Gardens 🚇 Lancaster Gate

QUEEN ALEXANDRA
This art nouveau bronze designed by Alfred Gilbert, a memorial to Edward VII's Danish-born wife, was commissioned by her daughter-in-law, Queen Mary.
✚ F6 ✉ Marlborough Road, SW1 🚇 Green Park

SIR ARTHUR SULLIVAN
William Goscombe John's bronze of the operetta composer Sir Arthur Sullivan (1842–1900).
✚ G5 ✉ Embankment Gardens 🚇 Embankment

BROADGATE CENTRE

Part of the rampant redevelopment of the City in the 1980s, Broadgate (➤ 56) was exceptional for its commissioning of public art. *Fulcrum* by Richard Serra–vast steel sheets tentatively resting against each other–marks the Broadgate square entrance. Beyond are Barry Flanagan's *Leaping Hare on Crescent and Bell* and George Segal's *Rush Hour*. In the center of Broadgate is the circular Arena, which becomes an outdoor ice rink in winter. Around its edge are chic restaurants, wine bars, and some shops.

Peter Pan in Kensington Gardens

New & Renovated Buildings

DESIGNER STORE INTERIORS

Sophisticated consumers have inspired retailers to create a stylish ambience in which to shop. Eva Jíricna has remodeled the Joseph shops (✉ 16 and 26 Sloane Street, SW1 and others) with her signature staircase, cable balustrades, and polished white plaster walls. Stanton Williams revamped Issey Miyake (✉ 270 Brompton Road, SW3), Branson Coates did Katharine Hamnett (✉ 20 Sloane Square, SW1) and Jigsaw (✉ 9 Argyll Street, W1 and others), and Wickham & Associates made Fifth Floor Harvey Nichols (➤ 73) a foodie's wonderland.

Broadgate

BROADGATE

This 29-acre mall and office development (1984–91) is distinguished by its impressive facades, street sculptures, open-air ice rink (Oct–Apr), and lunchtime events (summer). The architects were Arup Associates, Skidmore, Owings & Merrill, Inc. (➤ 55 panel).

✚ K4 ✉ EC2 ☎ 020 7505 4000 ⏰ 24 hours 🍴 Many 🚇 Liverpool Street

BRITISH LIBRARY

Colin St. John Wilson's redbrick home (1998) for the nation's books, with public galleries and piazza.

✚ G3 ✉ 96 Euston Road, NW1 ☎ 020 7412 7000 ⏰ Mon, Wed, Thu, Fri 9:30–6; Tue 9:30–8; Fri, Sat 9:30–5; Sun 11–5 🍴 Café, restaurant 🚇 Kings Cross 🎫 Free 🔗 Millennium Bridge and Millennium Dome (➤ 59)

BRITISH MUSEUM

Foster and Partners have created the Great Court (1998), a glass-roofed central courtyard with new amenities that make the BM the most pleasing national museum to visit anywhere (details ➤ 45).

CANARY WHARF

César Pelli's soaring, blue-topped tower (1991)—the first to be clad in stainless steel—dominates Canary Wharf; Pelli describes it as "a square prism with pyramidal top in the traditional form of the obelisk." Buildings by other international architects surround it.

✚ Off map at N6 ✉ 1 Canada Square, Canary Wharf, Isle of Dogs, E14 ⏰ Public spaces are open, not buildings 🚇 Canary Wharf

ROYAL OPERA HOUSE

Dixon Jones and BDP have created three theaters and a huge lobby (opened 1999) on a large site, incorporating the old opera house and Floral Hall.

✚ G5 ✉ Bow Street, WC2 ☎ 020 7304 4000 ⏰ All day 🍴 Café 🎫 Free; charge for tours 🚇 Covent Garden

WATERLOO INTERNATIONAL STATION

Designed by Nicholas Grimshaw and Partners and built to handle up to 15 million passengers a year, this is one of the world's longest railroad stations. The viaduct structure for five new tracks is spanned by a dramatic, glazed bowstring arch (1991–93).

✚ H6 ✉ SE1 ⏰ Public space 🍴 Many 🚇 Waterloo

WELLINGTON ARCH

Decimus Burton's great gateway, built 1827–28, topped by London's largest bronze sculpture, Victory (1912), is restored and contains exhibitions.

✚ E6 ✉ Hyde Park Corner, SW1 ☎ 020 7930 2726 ⏰ Wed–Sun 10–6 🎫 Moderate 🚇 Hyde Park Corner

Churches & Cathedrals

CHAPELS ROYAL

London's five Chapels Royal are at St. James's Palace, Queen's Chapel, the Tower (St. Peter ad Vincula and St. John's), and Hampton Court Palace. The best services to attend are at St. Peter ad Vincula, St. James's Palace, and Hampton Court, as each retains a lavish, courtly atmosphere and has a superb choir.

ALL-HALLOWS-BY-THE-TOWER

Begun about 1000, the church contains a Roman pavement and a carving by Grinling Gibbons.
➕ K5 ✉ Byward Street, EC3 ☎ 020 7481 2928 🕐 Church Mon–Fri 9–6; Sat 10–6; Sun 11–5 🚇 Tower Hill 💷 Charge for self-guiding audio tour

HOLY TRINITY, SLOANE STREET

Late Gothic Revival church with glorious Arts and Crafts interior and glass by Burne-Jones, William Morris, and others.
➕ E7 ✉ Sloane Street, SW1 ☎ 020 7235 3383 🕐 Mon–Fri; Sun services 🚇 Sloane Square 💷 Donation

ORATORY OF ST. PHILIP NERI

Also known as the Brompton or London Oratory (1876). Fine baroque interior.
➕ D7 ✉ Brompton Road, SW7 ☎ 020 7808 0900 🕐 Daily 6:30AM–8PM 🚇 South Kensington 💷 Donation

ST. JAMES'S, PICCADILLY

Wren's chic church (1682–84) for local aristocracy has a sumptuous interior.
➕ F6 ✉ Piccadilly, SW1 ☎ 020 7734 4511 🕐 Apr–Sep: daily 8–7. Oct–Mar: daily 9–6 🍴 Café 🚇 Piccadilly Circus 💷 Donation

ST. MARGARET, LOTHBURY

Wren's church (1686–90) retains its huge carved screen with soaring eagle and carved pulpit tester.
➕ J5 ✉ Lothbury, EC2 ☎ 020 7606 8330 🕐 Mon–Fri 8–5 🚇 Bank 💷 Donation

SOUTHWARK CATHEDRAL

Atmospheric of its medieval origins, despite much rebuilding; fine choir and monuments.
➕ J6 ✉ Montague Close, SE1 ☎ 020 7367 6700 🕐 Daily 8–6 🚇 London Bridge 🚉 London Bridge 💷 Donation

TEMPLE CHURCH

Begun about 1160, this private chapel has a circular plan inspired by Jerusalem's Dome of the Rock. Effigies honor the Knights Templar, protectors of pilgrims to the Holy Land.
➕ H5 ✉ Inner Temple, EC4 ☎ 020 7353 3470 🕐 Wed–Sat 11–4; Sun services. Closed for private functions 🚇 Temple 💷 Donation

The Oratory of St. Philip Neri (Brompton Oratory), by Herbert Gribble (1876)

Green Spaces

London is almost 11 percent parkland and has 67 square miles of green space, including the nine royal parks, former royal hunting grounds.

┌─ **In the Top 25** ─────────────────────────┐
6 HAMPSTEAD HEATH (► 31)
2 KENSINGTON GARDENS (► 27)
7 REGENT'S PARK (► 32)
1 ROYAL BOTANICAL GARDENS, KEW (► 26)
10 ST. JAMES'S PARK (► 35)
└───┘

BUNHILL FIELDS
Leafy City oasis, where trees shade the tombs of William Blake and Daniel Defoe.
✚ J4 ✉ City Road, EC1 ◷ Daily 7:30–dusk ◉ Old Street ✋ Free

Riders in Rotten Row, Hyde Park

GREEN PARK
Peaceful royal park.
✚ F6 ✉ SW1 ☎ 020 7930 1793 ◷ Daily dawn–dusk ◉ Green Park or Hyde Park Corner ✋ Free

GREENWICH (► 20)

HOLLAND PARK
Woodland and open lawns fill 54 acres around Holland House.
✚ A6 ✉ W11 ☎ 020 7471 9813 ◷ Daily 8–dusk ⁌ Restaurant, café ◉ Holland Park ✋ Free

HOLY TRINITY, BROMPTON
A large, tree-shaded, airy churchyard, useful between South Kensington Museum visits.
✚ D7 ✉ Brompton Road, SW7 ◷ 24 hours ◉ South Kensington ✋ Free

ROYAL PARKS

The nine royal parks, mostly former hunting grounds, are Londoners' substitute backyards. They act as the city's green lungs and many are also important bird sanctuaries. Their open spaces, woods, meadows, ponds, and wide variety of mature trees have been the setting for events ranging from the Great Exhibition of 1851 to riotous demonstrations. Today, they are places to meet, picnic, play games and, in summer, enjoy a concert or a play.

HYDE PARK
One of London's largest open spaces, tamed by 18th-century royalty.
✚ D6 ✉ W2 ☎ 020 7298 2000 ◷ Daily 5–midnight ⁌ Restaurant, café ◉ Marble Arch, Lancaster Gate, Knightsbridge, or Hyde Park Corner ✋ Free

PRIMROSE HILL
One of London's best panoramas.
✚ D2 ✉ NW3 ☎ 020 7486 7905 ◷ Daily dawn–9PM ◉ St. John's Wood or Camden Town ✋ Free

RUSSELL SQUARE
Lawns, trees, and café near the British Museum.
✚ G4 ✉ WC1 ◷ Daily 7–dusk ⁌ Café ◉ Russell Square ✋ Free

Thames Sights

London grew up around the Thames. As the port expanded, so did London's wealth and power. The Thames was its main thoroughfare, used by all.

In the Top 25

25 **H.M. THE TOWER OF LONDON (➤ 50)**
15 **HOUSES OF PARLIAMENT (➤ 38)**
1 **ROYAL BOTANICAL GARDENS, KEW (➤ 26)**
18 **SOMERSET HOUSE (➤ 43)**
11 22 **TATE GALLERIES (➤ 36, 47)**

BRITISH AIRWAYS LONDON EYE (➤ 60)

CLEOPATRA'S NEEDLE
The 86-foot pink-granite obelisk made in 1450 BC records the triumphs of Rameses the Great.
✚ G6 ✉ Victoria Embankment, WC2 🚇 Embankment or Charing Cross 🎫 Free

DOCKLANDS
Waterparks, the high-level Docklands Light Railway, Island Gardens, Museum in Docklands, and more.
✉ Stretches eastward from Tower of London to Royal Docks 🕐 24 hours for public areas 🚇 Use DLR to explore 🎫 Free

DRAGONS ON THE EMBANKMENT
The silver cast-iron dragons (1849) mark the City of London boundary.
✚ H5 ✉ Victoria Embankment, WC2 🚇 Temple

MILLENNIUM DOME
Richard Rogers and Partners' huge land-mark dome (➤ 15) at Greenwich Peninsula is closed but there are good views by boat.
✚ Off map at N8 ✉ Greenwich Peninsula, SE10 ☎ Information 020 8858 6376 🚢 Riverboat to the Thames Barrier

TOWER BRIDGE EXPERIENCE
Opened in 1894; fine views from the museum and catwalk between the tow-ers; engine rooms at the south bank end.
✚ K6 ✉ Tower Bridge, SE1 ☎ 020 7403 3761 🕐 Apr–Oct: daily 10–6:30. Nov–Mar: daily 9:30–6. Last admission 75 minutes before closing 🚇 Tower Hill 🚢 Riverboat to Tower Pier 🎫 Expensive

WATERLOO & MILLENNIUM BRIDGES
Gilbert Scott's mid-19th century cantilevered concrete, and Caro and Rogers' 2000 superfine span (➤ 15), both with great views.
Waterloo Bridge ✚ H6 ✉ WC2 🚇 Waterloo
Millennium Bridge ✚ J5–J6 ✉ EC4 🚇 Mansion House

RIVERBOATS

On a sunny day, take the underground to Westminster and catch a riverboat up or down the Thames for the morning. Trips downstream pass Westminster, the City, and Docklands, stopping at several piers. A longer trip upstream meanders past London's villages, stopping at Putney Bridge, Kew, Richmond, and Hampton Court piers.

The Prospect of Whitby, an old riverside smugglers' pub in Wapping

Family Favorites

BACKSTAGE TOURS

Going behind the scenes is great fun. In London, there are some excellent backstage tours. See how the scenery, props, and costumes are made at the National Theatre (► 81), or explore backstage at the Royal Shakespeare Company's Barbican and Pit theaters (► 81) and the Royal Opera House (► 56). Sports-keen kids can join tours of the MCC at Lord's (► 62 panel), Rugby Football Union Stadium at Twickenham (☎ 020 8892 8877), and Wimbledon Lawn Tennis Club (☎ 020 8944 1066). Reservations recommended for all.

Bethnal Green Museum of Childhood

BETHNAL GREEN MUSEUM OF CHILDHOOD

This outpost of the Victoria & Albert Museum (► 30) is an enormous train shed packed with Noah's arks, dolls, toy soldiers, puppets, and even a model circus.

➕ M3 ✉ Cambridge Heath Road, E2 ☎ 020 8983 5200/2415 🕐 Sun–Thu, Sat 10–5:30 🍴 Café 🚇 Bethnal Green 🚋 Bethnal Green 💷 Free

BRITISH AIRWAYS LONDON EYE

A 30-minute ride on the world's tallest observation wheel; a fabulous bird's eye view of London.

➕ G6 ✉ Jubilee Gardens, SE1 ☎ 0870 500 0600 🕐 Jun–Aug: daily 10–10. Apr, May, Sep: daily 1–8. Oct–Mar: daily 10–7 🚇 Waterloo or Westminster 💷 Expensive

FIREPOWER

The Royal Artillery collections, ranging from Roman trebuchets to an Iraqi supergun, plus models, uniforms, and plenty of visitor participation.

➕ Off the map from H7 ✉ The Royal Arsenal, Woolwich, SE18 ☎ 0208 8854 0916/8855 7755 🕐 Daily 10–5 🚇 Woolwich Arsenal 🚢 Ferry from Greenwich 💷 Moderate

HAMLEYS

An everlasting favorite, a tourist attraction in its own right, and five floors packed with toys and crowds. Huge selection of board games and a video arcade in the basement. High prices.

➕ F5 ✉ 188–196 Regent Street, W1 ☎ 020 7494 2000 🕐 Mon–Fri 10–8; Sat 9:30–8; Sun noon–6 🚇 Oxford Circus 💷 Free

HANDEL HOUSE MUSEUM

Anyone who plays a muscial instrument or sings "The Messiah" at Christmas should not miss a visit to the composer's London home from 1723 until 1759.

➕ E5 ✉ 25 Brook Street, W1 ☎ 0207 7495 1685 🕐 Tue, Wed–Sat 10–6; Thu 10–8; Sun noon–6 🚇 Bond Street or Oxford Circus 💷 Moderate

H.M.S. *BELFAST*

Put aside two hours to clamber up, down, and around this 1938 war cruiser, visiting the cabins, gun turrets, bridge, and boiler-room. One of the most spectacular sights on the River Thames.

➕ K6 ✉ Morgan's Lane, Tooley Street, SE1 ☎ 020 7940 6300 🕐 Mar–Oct: daily 10–6. Nov–Feb: daily 10–5 🍴 Café 🚇 London Bridge 🚋 London Bridge 💷 Moderate; family ticket

IMAX CINEMAS

London's two gargantuan screens are at the Wellcome Wing of the Science Museum (➤ 29), and on the South Bank.

✚ G6 ✉ BFI London IMAX Cinema, 1 Charlie Chaplin Walk, South Bank, SE1 ☎ 020 7902 1234 ⏰ Daily noon–8:30. Late shows Fri, Sat 🚇 Waterloo 🚃 Waterloo 💷 Moderate

MADAME TUSSAUD'S & THE LONDON PLANETARIUM

Madame Tussaud learned the art of waxworks from her uncle; see how many people you can identify, from Shakespeare to Madonna, and do not miss the Spirit of London ride. The Planetarium has good star shows and an interactive exhibition area.

✚ E4 ✉ Marylebone Road, W1 ☎ 020 7935 6861 ⏰ May–Sep: daily 9:30–5:30. Oct–April: Mon–Fri 10–5:30; Sat, Sun 9:30–5:30. Planetarium various, phone for current details 🍴 Restaurant, café 🚇 Baker Street 💷 Very expensive; family ticket; Tussaud's/ Planetarium combined ticket. Discount tickets for Rock Circus (below) available

THE ORIGINAL LONDON SIGHTSEEING TOUR

Cruise about town on an open-top double-decker bus whose five routes cover 80 stops; tickets and route maps available on board.

✚ Moves around central London ✉ Pick-up points include Victoria Street, Haymarket, Marble Arch, Strand, Charing Cross Pier ☎ 020 8877 1722 ⏰ Daily 8:30–6; departures every 10 minutes approximately 💷 Very expensive. Ticket valid 24 hours

ROCK CIRCUS

Music legends from Mick Jagger to Jamiroquai seem to come alive when visitors' headphones pick up infrared signals and play their songs.

✚ F5 ✉ London Pavilion, Piccadilly Circus, W1 ☎ 020 7734 7203 ⏰ Mar–Aug: Mon, Wed, Thu, Sun 10–8; Tue 11–8; Fri, Sat 10–9. Sep–Feb: Mon, Wed–Sun 10–5:30; Tue 11–5:30 🚇 Piccadilly Circus 💷 Very expensive; family ticket. Discount tickets for Madame Tussaud's

TOY WORLD, HARRODS

Up on the fourth floor, this is every child's dream outing. Plenty of toys for children to play with.

✚ D7 ✉ Brompton Road, SW1 ☎ 020 7730 1234 ⏰ Mon–Sat 10–7 🍴 Restaurants, cafés 🚇 Knightsbridge 💷 Free

W.W.T. WETLAND CENTRE

The well-established Wildfowl and Wetlands Trust opened its first London conservation area in 2000, 104 acres of lakes, ponds, grasslands, and mudflats that attract an abundance of wildlife.

✚ Off the map to southwest ✉ Queen Elizabeth's Walk, SW13 ☎ 020 8409 4400 ⏰ Apr–Sep: daily 9:30–6. Oct–Mar: daily 9:30–5; last admission 1 hour before closing 🚇 Hammersmith, then bus 33, 72, 209, 283 💷 Expensive

Harrods—an outing in itself

LONDON FOR FREE

London has plenty of free activities for all ages. Several public galleries are free (National Gallery ➤ 41, National Portrait Gallery ➤ 40, Tate Galleries, free except for special exhibitions ➤ 36, 47) plus the commercial ones (➤ 75). Many museums are free and music can be enjoyed in church concerts, pubs, and arts complexes. For free theater, try an art auction (➤ 75), a debate in Parliament (➤ 38), or a BBC recording session (☎ 020 8743 8000 and ask for ticket inquiries, specifying radio or TV).

Hidden London

───── In the Top 25 ─────
14 BANQUETING HOUSE (➤ 39)

CRICKET

Anyone who watches or plays cricket should visit the MCC Museum hidden away at Lord's. The story of the game is told in pictures, cartoons, and old battered bats; the Ashes are kept here, too. It is open to ticket-holders on match days, while at other times the guided tour includes the Long Room and the beautiful new stand designed by Michael Hopkins in 1985–87. ✚ D3 ✉ Marylebone Cricket Club, Lord's Ground, NW8 ☎ 020 7289 1611. Tour bookings 020 7432 1033 🕐 Guided tours, phone for availability 🚇 St. John's Wood 💷 Expensive

CHELSEA PHYSIC GARDEN
Sir Hans Sloane laid out this walled garden for the Society of Apothecaries in 1673.
✚ D8 ✉ Swan Walk, SW3 ☎ 020 7352 5646 🕐 Apr–Oct: Wed noon–5; Sun (usually) 2–6 🚇 Sloane Square 💷 Moderate

INNER AND MIDDLE TEMPLE
These two Inns of Court are named after the Knights Templar, whose church (➤ 57) is here, too.
✚ H5 ✉ Middle Temple, Middle Temple Lane, EC4
☎ 020 7427 4800 🕐 Middle Temple Hall Mon–Fri 10–11:30, 3–4:30 (phone first). Closed Aug and public hols 🚇 Temple 💷 Free

ROYAL HOSPITAL, CHELSEA
Wren's 1682 building, inspired by the Hôtel des Invalides in Paris, is still a home for veteran soldiers.
✚ E8 ✉ Royal Hospital Road, SW3 ☎ 020 7730 5282 🕐 Museum, Great Hall, and Chapel Mon–Fri 10–noon, 2–4; Sat 2–4; Sun opening May–Sep:2–4. Sun service 10:40. Closed May 15 to end Jun and public hols 🚇 Sloane Square 💷 Free

SPENCER HOUSE
Lavishly restored Palladian mansion, a rare survivor of 18th-century aristocratic St. James's and Mayfair.
✚ F6 ✉ 27 St. James's Place, SW1 🕐 Feb–Jul, Sep–Dec: Sun 11:45–4:45; booking advised, compulsory guided tour 🚇 Green Park 💷 Expensive; no children

TEMPLE OF MITHRAS
The ground floor of this Roman temple survives, relocated to the public pavement.
✚ J5 ✉ Bucklersbury, EC4 🕐 24 hours 🚇 Bank 💷 Free

VINOPOLIS
A warren of atmospheric rooms devoted to the world's wine-growing regions, with movies, experts, and plenty of tastings.
✚ J6 ✉ 1 Bank End, SE1 🕐 Mon 11–9; Tue–Fri, Sun 11–6; Sat 11–8; last admission 2 hours before closing 🚇 London Bridge 🚉 London Bridge 💷 Expensive, includes audio-guide and tastings

2 WILLOW ROAD
Designer Erno Goldfinger's striking home, built in 1939, complete with its contents. Guided tours only.
✚ Off the map ✉ 22 Willow Road, NW3 ☎ 020 7435 6166 🕐 Apr–Oct: Thu–Sat noon–5. Mar, Nov–Dec 15: noon–5 🚇 Hampstead 💷 Moderate

Chelsea Pensioners, residents of the Royal Hospital, Chelsea

LONDON
where to

English Restaurants

PRICES

Eating out in London is generally expensive and prices vary widely. In the restaurants listed on these pages, expect to pay per person for a meal (including drinks):

$ under £30
$$ £30–45
$$$ more than £45

When the check arrives, look it over carefully as a service charge (usually 10–12½ percent) and sometimes cover charges (approximately £2 per person) may be added. Check beforehand whether VAT and coffee are also included, and order tap water if you do not want to pay for bottled. A good-value menu can be transformed into an outrageous check if you do not look sharp. You are not obliged to leave a tip if service is added even if the credit card slip is left open.

ENGLISH CUISINE

English cuisine should no longer be derided; there is both fine traditional and impressive new wave cooking to be enjoyed.

ALASTAIR LITTLE: LANCASTER ROAD ($$)

If Alastair Little's plate-glass Soho showpiece is beyond the purse, come to this less formal but highly fashionable outpost.
➕ A5 ✉ 136a Lancaster Road, W11 ☎ 020 7243 2220 🕐 Mon–Sat lunch, dinner 🚇 Ladbroke Grove

AMPHITHEATRE ($$)

Excellent British food in the re-invented Royal Opera House complex, best for lunch at an outside table.
➕ G5 ✉ Covent Garden, WC2 ☎ 020 7212 9254 🕐 Mon–Fri lunch open to all; dinner open to opera ticket holders only 🚇 Covent Garden

AXIS ($$$)

Discreet, efficient, and sophisticated setting for imaginative modern British food; hovers between the West End and the City.
➕ G5 ✉ 1 Aldwych, WC2 ☎ 020 7300 0300 🕐 Mon–Fri lunch; Mon–Sat dinner 🚇 Covent Garden

THE GLASSHOUSE ($$)

The perfect preamble to a walk in Kew Gardens (➤ 26). Reserve to enjoy notable modern dishes right beside Kew station.
➕ Off the map from A8 ✉ 14 Station Parade, Kew ☎ 020 8940 6777 🕐 Daily lunch; Mon–Sat dinner 🚇 Kew Gardens

THE IVY ($$$)

A revived theaterland classic with artworks by Peter Blake and Howard Hodgkin on the walls, celebrities galore, and modern English food.

Reservations essential.
➕ G5 ✉ 1 West Street, WC2 ☎ 020 7836 4751 🕐 Lunch, dinner 🚇 Leicester Square

RULES ($$)

One of London's oldest restaurants, founded in 1798, serves good traditional English dishes in plush Edwardian rooms.
➕ G5 ✉ 35 Maiden Lane, WC2 ☎ 020 7836 5314 🕐 Lunch, dinner 🚇 Covent Garden

SIMPSON'S ($$)

Opened in 1848 as Simpson's Divan and Tavern, where chess players lolled on divans to feast on roast beef. Today, there's just the roast beef and other traditional dishes. Dress code: jacket and tie.
➕ G5 ✉ 110 Strand, WC2 ☎ 020 7836 9112 🕐 Lunch, dinner 🚇 Charing Cross

THE SUGAR CLUB ($$$)

Despite the departure of its founder, Peter Gordon, you will find gloriously inventive cooking in the minimalist setting.
➕ F5 ✉ 21 Warwick Street, W1 ☎ 020 7437 7776 🕐 Lunch, dinner 🚇 Piccadilly Circus

ST. JOHN ($$)

A short walk from the Barbican Centre, the robust English dishes range from rabbit and oxtail to serious puddings. Plenty of offal.
➕ J4 ✉ 26 St. John's Street, EC1 ☎ 020 7251 0848 🕐 Mon–Sat lunch, dinner 🚇 Barbican or Farringdon

Italian & French Restaurants

THE ADMIRALTY ($$)
Oliver Peyton's restaurant empire grows with this stunning site, serving modern continental dishes.
✚ H5 ✉ Somerset House, WC2 ☎ 020 7845 4646 ⏰ Daily lunch: Mon–Sat dinner 🚇 Temple

AL SAN VINCENZO ($$)
It is essential to reserve a table to enjoy Neapolitan Signore Borgonzolo's cooking.
✚ D5 ✉ 30 Connaught Street, W2 ☎ 020 7262 9623 ⏰ Mon–Fri lunch; Mon–Sat dinner 🚇 Marble Arch

ASSAGGI ($$)
Popular Italian above the Chepstow pub specializing in a dozen or so starters called *assaggi* (little tastes). Reserve well in advance.
✚ B5 ✉ The Chepstow, 39 Chepstow Place, W2 ☎ 020 7792 5501 ⏰ Lunch, dinner 🚇 Westbourne Park

CAFÉ DU MARCHÉ ($$)
In the cobblestone mews in the square's west corner, this rustic French restaurant has a laid-back pianist each evening.
✚ J4 ✉ 22 Charterhouse Square, EC1 ☎ 020 7608 1609 ⏰ Mon–Fri lunch; Mon–Sat dinner 🚇 Barbican

CLUB GASCON ($$)
Unusual, robust dishes from Gascony, with a good atmosphere; good for City or post-Barbican Centre dinner. Reserve well in advance.
✚ J4 ✉ 57 West Smithfield, EC1 ☎ 020 7796 0600 ⏰ Mon–Fri lunch, dinner 🚇 Barbican or St. Paul's

L'ESCARGOT ($$)
Stylish brasserie, a true Soho landmark, serving modern French cooking.
✚ G5 ✉ 48 Greek Street, W1 ☎ 020 7437 2679 ⏰ Mon–Fri lunch; Mon–Sat dinner 🚇 Leicester Square

MIMMO D'ISHCIA ($$$)
Long-established Belgravia haunt favored by locals; guaranteed good atmosphere; big-bowl pasta dishes keep the check in line.
✚ E7 ✉ 61 Elizabeth Street, SW1 ☎ 020 7730 5406 ⏰ Daily lunch; Mon–Sat dinner 🚇 Sloane Street or Victoria

PALAIS DU JARDIN ($$)
Congenial atmosphere and food in a huge, smart brasserie, with tables outside in summer.
✚ G5 ✉ 136 Long Acre, WC2 ☎ 020 7379 5353 ⏰ Lunch, dinner 🚇 Leicester Square or Covent Garden

MIRABELLE ($$$)
Ultra glamorous setting for a top notch modern classic French restaurant with an exceptional wine list.
✚ E6 ✉ 56 Curzon Street, W1 ☎ 020 7499 4636 ⏰ Lunch, dinner 🚇 Green Park

ZAFFERANO ($$$)
Giorgio Locatelli specializes in modern interpretations of simple Italian country cooking. Sharp service; reservations essential.
✚ D7 ✉ 16 Lowndes Street, SW1 ☎ 020 7235 5800 ⏰ Mon–Sat lunch, dinner 🚇 Knightsbridge

SET-PRICE MENUS
Many of London's pricier restaurants offer two set-price menus serving sublime dishes–lower in price at lunchtime. Consider dressing up to try classic Anglo-French cuisine at the exquisite Connaught Grill (✚ E5 ✉ 16 Carlos Place, W1 ☎ 020 7499 7070) or spend an afternoon lunching at Gordon Ramsey's restaurant (▶ 68). Most of the star chefs offer these menus, from Alastair Little (▶ 64) and Richard Corrigan to Philip Howard, Jean-Christophe Novelli, and Michel Roux (all ▶ 68).

Asian Restaurants

INDIAN FOOD

London's 2,000 or so Indian restaurants cater to a well-informed local clientele, so this is a good moment to visit one. An Indian meal should have many dishes so, if you are a group, consider making a collective order and sharing. Tandoori dishes (cooked in a clay oven) make good starters. Main course dishes should arrive together and include one or two meat offerings, two or three vegetable dishes, rice, a lentil, or pulse serving (such as chickpeas), and a variety of breads such as *chapati* or *naan*—which are eaten hot, so order more as you go along. Remember the yogurt and pickles, and drink *lassi* (sweet or salty variations on buttermilk/yogurt) or beer. Vegetarians will find a good range of mild and spicy food.

CHOR BIZARRE ($$)
Slow service, but worth the wait for delicious Indian food including some unusual regional dishes.
➕ F6 ✉ 16 Albermarle Street, W1 ☎ 020 7629 9802
🕐 Lunch, dinner 🚇 Green Park

CHUTNEYS ($)
An informal good-value stop in this street known for its Indian food.
➕ F4 ✉ 124 Drummond Street, NW1 ☎ 020 7388 0604 🕐 Lunch daily, dinner Mon–Sat 🚇 Euston Square or Warren Street

MASALA ZONE ($)
From the creators of Chutney Mary and Veeraswamy, both loved for their authentic dishes, comes an informal setting for the distinctive Gujarati meals of western India.
➕ F5 ✉ 9 Marshall Street, W1 ☎ 020 787 9966 🕐 Lunch, dinner 🚇 Oxford Circus

NOBU ($$$)
New York's Nobuyuki Matsuhisa brings his pan-American Japanese cooking to London. Equally pricey outpost Ubon, at Canary Wharf.
➕ E6 ✉ Metropolitan Hotel, 19 Old Park Lane, W1 ☎ 020 7447 4747 🕐 Mon–Fri lunch, dinner 🚇 Hyde Park Corner

RASA ($)
Inspired Keralan cooking, one of India's softer cuisines.
➕ E5 ✉ 6 Dering Street, W1 ☎ 020 7629 1346
🕐 Mon–Sat lunch, dinner 🚇 Bond Street

ROYAL CHINA ($$)
Reserve a table or join the justifiably long lines for the best dim sum in town. Three branches.
➕ C5 ✉ 13 Queensway, W2 ☎ 020 7221 2535 🕐 Sat, Sun lunch, dinner 🚇 Queensway

SALLOOS ($$)
Consistently perfect Pakistani dishes from the North-Western Frontier, ideal for good appetites and meat lovers.
➕ E7 ✉ 62–64 Kinnerton Street, SW1 ☎ 020 7235 4444 🕐 Mon–Sat lunch, dinner 🚇 Knightsbridge

SHOGUN ($$$)
Expensive, but worth it for the authentic dishes and—rare in London's Japanese restaurants—good atmosphere.
➕ E5 ✉ Adam's Row, W1 ☎ 020 7493 1255 🕐 Tue–Sat dinner 🚇 Bond Street

TAMARIND ($$)
Delicious traditional village dishes from Uttar Prades, Kerala, and other Indian states.
➕ E6 ✉ 20 Queen Street, W1 ☎ 020 7629 3561 🕐 Sun–Fri lunch; dinner daily 🚇 Green Park

TATSUSO ($$$)
For City budgets only, the best Japanese in town: *tappen-yaki* upstairs and sushi downstairs.
➕ K4 ✉ 32 Broadgate Circle EC2 ☎ 020 7638 5863 🕐 Mon–Fri lunch, dinner 🚇 Liverpool Street

WAGAMAMA ($)
Trendy Japanese *ramen* bar near the British Museum. Five branches; no reservations.
➕ G5 ✉ 4 Streatham Street, WC1 ☎ 020 7323 9223 🕐 Lunch, dinner 🚇 Tottenham Court Road

Fish & Vegetarian Restaurants

BACK TO BASICS ($$)

Modestly priced, imaginative fish dishes in an unpretentious bistro a short walk from the British Museum or Oxford Street.

🟦 F4 ✉ 21a Foley Street, W1 ☎ 020 7436 2181 🕐 Mon–Fri lunch, dinner 🚇 Goodge Street

BANK ($$)

Dramatic modern brasserie setting for excellent fish dishes, from "fish and chips" to lobster.

🟦 G5 ✉ 1 Kingsway, WC2 ☎ 020 7379 9797 🕐 Lunch, dinner 🚇 Covent Garden

CARNEVALE ($)

Inventive dishes at this little Clerkenwell restaurant, ideal post City sight-seeing or pre-Barbican.

🟦 J4 ✉ 135 Whitecross Street, EC1 ☎ 020 7250 3452 🕐 Mon–Fri lunch; Mon–Sat dinner 🚇 Old Street

DIWANA BHEL POORI HOUSE ($)

Bhel poori are fried snacks sold on Bombay streets and beaches; in this vegetarian restaurant they are served as first courses.

🟦 F4 ✉ 121 Drummond Street, NW1 ☎ 020 7387 5556 🕐 Lunch buffet, dinner (bring your own alcohol) 🚇 Euston

THE GATE ($)

Imaginative vegetarian food and an often-changing menu mean reserving is essential at this useful pre-show Hammersmith hideaway.

🟦 Off the map from A7 ✉ 51 Queen Caroline Street, W6 ☎ 020 8748 6932 🕐 Mon–Fri lunch; Mon–Sat dinner 🚇 Hammersmith

LIVEBAIT ($$)

From its original near the Young and Old Vic theaters in The Cut, success has spawned Livebait fish restaurants in Covent Garden and Notting Hill—so far.

🟦 H6 ✉ 43 The Cut, SE1 ☎ 020 7928 7211 🕐 Mon–Sat lunch, dinner 🚇 Southwark

THE PLACE BELOW ($)

Exceptional vegetarian food in an ancient Norman church crypt in the heart of the City.

🟦 J5 ✉ St. Mary-le-Bow, Cheapside, EC2 ☎ 020 7329 0789 🕐 Mon–Fri lunch 🚇 St. Paul's or Bank

J. SHEEKEY ($$)

Renovated and re-invigorated by The Ivy/Caprice team, with its traditional fish dishes correspondingly refined.

🟦 G5 ✉ 28–32 St. Martin's Court, WC2 ☎ 020 7240 2565 🕐 Mon–Sat lunch, Mon–Fri dinner 🚇 Leicester Square

SWEETINGS ($$)

Unashamedly old-fashioned City fish parlor; no reservations, so arrive early or late if you want a table.

🟦 J5 ✉ 39 Queen Victoria Street, EC4 ☎ 020 7248 3062 🕐 Mon–Fri lunch 🚇 Mansion House

WORLD FOOD CAFÉ ($)

A fresh, modern approach to vegetarian food, with Indian, Mexican, Greek, and Turkish influences.

🟦 G5 ✉ 14 Neal's Yard, WC2 ☎ 020 7379 0298 🕐 Mon–Fri noon–4:30; Sat noon–5 🚇 Covent Garden

ROMANTIC EATING

If it is the setting that is important for your "dinner a deux," consider going traditional and grand at The Ritz or the Savoy River Room. For something more dramatic and modern, the Oxo Tower's restaurant or brasserie, or the top floor of the Tate Modern might be right; both have fantastic views. If the French atmosphere is essential, try the intimate and fairly modest La Poule au Pot, or perhaps Julie's. Match romance with modern British cooking at the sumptuous Launceston Place, the spoiling Odette's, or the more clubby and high fashion Le Caprice.

VEGETARIAN EATING

Vegetarians are well catered for in London. Most restaurants offer a range of non-meat and non-fish meals, while Indian cooking is famed for its imaginative vegetable and pulse dishes. If fish remains an option, the capital has a wide range on offer.

Famous Chefs

RICHARD CORRIGAN: LINDSAY HOUSE ($$$)

Inspired modern British cooking in a delightful Soho townhouse.

G5 ✉ 21 Romilly Street, W1 ☎ 020 7439 0450 🕐 Mon–Fri lunch; Mon–Sat dinner 🚇 Piccadilly Circus

PHILIP HOWARD: THE SQUARE ($$$)

Impressive modern French food matched by a chic, but formal Mayfair interior.

F5 ✉ 6 Bruton Street, W1 ☎ 020 7495 7100 🕐 Mon–Fri lunch; Mon–Sat dinner 🚇 Bond Street

BRUCE POOLE: CHEZ BRUCE ($$)

Worth the journey to Wandsworth Common to enjoy Poole's short menu of consistent and delicious modern British dishes, slick service, and fair prices.

Off the map from E10 ✉ 2 Bellevue Road, SW17 ☎ 020 8672 0114 🕐 Daily lunch; Mon–Sat dinner 🚇 Balham

JEAN-CHRISTOPHE NOVELLI: MAISON NOVELLI ($$$)

Well worth bypassing the brasserie for the pricier upstairs restaurant.

H4 ✉ 29 Clerkenwell Green, EC1 ☎ 020 7251 6606 🕐 Mon–Fri lunch, dinner 🚇 Farringdon

GORDON RAMSAY: GORDON RAMSAY RESTAURANT ($$$)

Breathtaking interpretation of French cooking; every detail of food, service, and formal setting perfect.

E8 ✉ 68 Royal Hospital Road, SW3 ☎ 020 7352 4441 🕐 Mon–Fri lunch, dinner 🚇 Sloane Square

ROBERT REID: THE OAK ROOM ($$$)

Opulent surroundings for cooking that is the ultimate in luxury and perfection. Marco Pierre White's departure means prices are less outrageous.

F5 ✉ Le Meridien Piccadilly, 21 Piccadilly W1 ☎ 020 7437 0202 🕐 Mon–Fri lunch, dinner 🚇 Piccadilly Circus

GARY RHODES: CITY RHODES ($$$)

With his stunning English cooking and sharp service, the charming Rhodes has wooed City lunchers; so reserve well ahead.

H5 ✉ New Street Square, EC4 ☎ 020 7583 1313 🕐 Mon–Fri lunch and early dinner (closes 9PM) 🚇 Chancery Lane

MICHEL ROUX: LA GAVROCHE ($$$)

Albert's son sticks to classic French, but lighter; amazing wines, grand setting.

E5 ✉ 43 Upper Brook Street, W1 ☎ 020 7408 0881 🕐 Mon–Sat lunch, dinner 🚇 Oxford Circus

MARCUS WAREING: PETRUS ($$$)

As the sister restaurant to Gordon Ramsey, Marcus Wareing offers a rich cocktail of powerful modern French food, fine wines, and traditional service.

F6 ✉ 33 St. James's Street, SW1 ☎ 020 7930 4272 🕐 Mon–Fri lunch; Mon–Sat dinner 🚇 Green Park

RIVERSIDE EATING

London is exploiting the potential of its riverside views. Today, there is more than just the grand Savoy River Room and the East End smugglers' pubs. The most spectacular views are from the Oxo Tower Restaurant (✉ Barge House Street, SE1) with its serious food–and prices–as well as Tate Modern's rooftop restaurant at Bankside (► 47). There are lower but impressive views from the second-floor Blue Print Café, beside the Design Museum, Butler's Wharf, overlooking Tower Bridge and the City (► 52). For more modest river-view eating, try Barley Mow pub (✉ 44 Narrow Street, E14), whose outdoor tables overlook the wider, curving Thames of the East End.

Breakfast & Tea

BANK ALDWYCH ($)

Great setting and superb breakfast to start a busy City or sightseeing day.
- ✚ G5 ✉ 1 Kingsway, WC2
- ☎ 020 7379 9797
- ⏱ Mon–Fri 7:30–10AM
- Ⓜ Covent Garden

BANK WESTMINSTER ($)

Fortify yourself before exploring Westminster.
- ✚ F7 ✉ Buckingham Gate, SW1 ☎ 020 7379 9797
- ⏱ Daily 6–10.30AM
- Ⓜ Victoria

BLISS ($)

Sumptuous croissants, *tartes au citron*, ideal pre- or post-Camden Passage (antiques).
- ✚ H3 ✉ 428 St. John Street, EC1 ☎ 020 7837 3720
- ⏱ Mon–Fri 8–6; Sat 8:30–6; Sun 9–5 Ⓜ Angel

BRITISH MUSEUM ($)

Take coffee and croissants at the Great Court's cafés to kick off your cultural day; late risers can have coffee and cakes at a window table in the sixth floor Court Restaurant.
- ✚ G4 ✉ Great Russell Street, WC1 ☎ 020 7323 8990
- ⏱ Cafés daily from 9AM; restaurant from 11AM
- Ⓜ Holborn or Goodge Street

CLARIDGE'S ($)

Breakfast is in the immaculate art deco restaurant; tea—among the best in London—is taken on sofas in the lobby alcove. Reservations essential. Dress code: jacket and tie.
- ✚ E5 ✉ Brook Street, W1
- ☎ 020 7629 8860
- ⏱ Breakfast, tea
- Ⓜ Bond Street

FOX & ANCHOR ($)

Join Smithfield meat market workers for a hearty old-fashioned breakfast and a beer.
- ✚ J4 ✉ 115 Charterhouse Street, EC1 ☎ 020 77253 5075
- ⏱ Mon–Fri 7AM–11PM
- Ⓜ Barbican or Farringdon

MANDARIN ORIENTAL HYDE PARK ($$)

The window tables in the lounge conservatory overlooking Hyde Park are the best for afternoon tea.
- ✚ E6 ✉ Knightsbridge, SW1 ☎ 020 7235 2000
- ⏱ Breakfast, tea Ⓜ Hyde Park Corner

PÂTISSERIE VALERIE ($)

Coffee, croissants, and delicious cakes at tiny tables in the original café-shop. Six branches.
- ✚ F5 ✉ 44 Old Compton Street, W1 ☎ 020 7437 3466
- ⏱ Breakfast, tea Ⓜ Leicester Square or Tottenham Court Road

PAUL ($)

Stunning patisserie, a branch of its French mother founded in 1889; hot chocolate, pastries, and savories that dreams are made of.
- ✚ G5 ✉ 29 Bedford Street, WC2 ☎ 020 7836 3304
- ⏱ Mon–Fri 7:30AM–9PM; Sat, Sun 9–9 Ⓜ Covent Garden

SIMPSON'S ($$)

Glorious setting for a traditional breakfast, such as porridge followed by kippers or kidneys. Dress code: jacket and tie.
- ✚ G5 ✉ 100 Strand, WC2
- ☎ 020 7836 9112
- ⏱ Breakfast, tea
- Ⓜ Charing Cross

BEST SETTINGS

If part of the pleasure of dining out is the setting try lunch or dinner at the Ritz (▶ 86); or perhaps the Savoy River Room ; the Coq d'Argent (1 Poultry, EC3); the Tate Modern (▶ 47); the National Portrait Gallery (▶ 40); or the British Museum's Court Restaurant (▶ 45, 56). Go to the mosaic-clad Criterion (✉ 224 Piccadilly, W1) for sparkle and Claridge's (▶ this page, 86) for Art Deco. Wacky settings include the Dorchester's pricey Oriental (✉ Park Lane, W1). For atmospheric pubs go to the George Inn (✉ 77 Borough High Street, SE1) or the Admiral Codrington (▶ 71). Bank (▶ 67) and Oxo Tower Restaurant (✉ Barge House Street, SE1) are architects' dreams. And you'll find the most beautiful walls at Christopher's (▶ 70). For a fabulous romantic setting try the Brew House restaurant at Kenwood House (▶ 31) with panoramic views over the sweeping gardens.

Brasseries & Brunch

THE AMERICAN EXPERIENCE

America's fast food arrived long before its quality cuisine and restaurant style became established. Upscale options include Joe Allen and Christopher's (both this page), and PJ's (✉ 52 Fulham Road, SW3). Other good-value places to hang out include:

Babe Ruth's ✉ 172–176 The Highway, E1 and 02 Centre, 255 Finchley Road, NW3

Arkansas Café ✉ Unit 12, Old Spitalfield Market, E1

Big Easy ✉ 1332–334 King's Road, SW3

The Hard Rock Café ✉ 150 Old Park Lane, W1

The Navajo Joe ✉ 134 King Street, WC2

Santa Fe ✉ 75 Upper Street, N1

Shoeless Joe's ✉ Temple Place, WC2 and 555 King's Road, SW6

TGI Friday's ✉ 6 Bedford Street (and branches)

LA BRASSERIE ($$)

Long established focus for Chelsea area singles to meet friends before cruising around Brompton Cross shops.

✚ D7 ✉ 272 Brompton Road, SW3 ☎ 020 7584 1668 ◐ Lunch, dinner ⊜ South Kensington

BRASSERIE DU MARCHÉ AUX PUCES ($$)

At the north end of Portobello Road; ideal after Portobello Market.

✚ B5 ✉ 349 Portobello Road, W10 ☎ 020 8968 5828 ◐ Breakfast, lunch, dinner ⊜ Ladbroke Grove

BRASSERIE ROQUE ($$)

Well-located City brasserie, with the benefit of outdoor tables in summer and, sometimes, music or entertainment.

✚ K4 ✉ 37 Broadgate Circle ☎ 020 7638 7919 ◐ Mon–Fri lunch ⊜ Liverpool Street

LA BRASSERIE ST. QUENTIN ($$)

Uncompromisingly French—great for an indulgent break from a South Kensington Museums day.

✚ D7 ✉ 243 Brompton Road, SW3 ☎ 020 7589 8005 ◐ Lunch, dinner ⊜ South Kensington

THE BRIDGE ($$)

Stunning views of the Millennium Bridge and Tate Modern, to be enjoyed with modern British food.

✚ J5 ✉ 11 Paul's Walk, EC4 ☎ 020 7236 0000 ◐ Daily lunch; Mon–Fri dinner ⊜ Mansion House

CAMDEN BRASSERIE ($$)

Good for grilled steak, *frites*, and a bottle of wine after Camden Lock markets.

✚ F2 ✉ 214–16 Camden High Street, NW1 ☎ 020 7482 2114 ◐ Lunch, dinner; Sun brunch ⊜ Camden Town

CHRISTOPHER'S ($$$)

One of the best London haunts for a genuine American brunch, and in one of the capital's most beautiful dining rooms.

✚ G5 ✉ 18 Wellington Street, WC2 ☎ 020 7240 4222 ◐ Lunch, dinner; Sat, Sun brunch ⊜ Covent Garden

DAKOTA ($$)

U.S. southwestern cooking that's a hit with cool locals. Best for brunch.

✚ B5 ✉ 127 Ledbury Road, W11 ☎ 020 7792 9191 ◐ Lunch, dinner ⊜ Notting Hill Gate

JOE ALLEN ($$)

Dependably convivial and club-like. Healthy American Cal-Ital food served by smiling waiters. Reservations essential.

✚ G5 ✉ 13 Exeter Street, WC2 ☎ 020 7836 0651 ◐ Lunch, dinner; Sat, Sun brunch ⊜ Covent Garden

UNION CAFE ($$)

Stylish, casual, very popular, simple appealing food and quality wines.

✚ E4 ✉ 96 Marylebone Lane, W1 ☎ 020 7486 4860 ◐ Mon–Sat breakfast, lunch, tea, dinner ⊜ Bond Street

Shops & Pubs

ADMIRAL CODRINGTON ($$)

Stylish Knightsbridge pub serving modern British food amid winter fires and summer sunshine.

➕ D7 ✉ 17 Mossop Street, SW3 ☎ 020 7581 0005
🕐 Lunch, dinner 🚇 High Street Kensington

CROSS KEYS ($$)

Old pub in the Chelsea lanes, great after a visit to the Royal Hospital; robust modern British food.

➕ D8 ✉ 1 Lawrence Street, SW3 ☎ 020 7349 9111
🕐 Lunch, dinner
🚇 Sloane Square

DUKE OF YORK ($)

Lunch is understandably packed in this dated, well-worn pub with its Mediterranean-inspired food.

➕ G4 ✉ 7 Roger Street, WC1 ☎ 020 7242 7230
🕐 Mon–Fri lunch; Mon–Sat dinner 🚇 Russell Square

THE EAGLE ($)

The first of London's new-wave pubs (opened 1991) serves robust, Mediterranean food to a noisy, full house.

➕ H4 ✉ 159 Farringdon Road, EC1 ☎ 020 7837 1353
🕐 Mon–Sat lunch, dinner
🚇 Farringdon

THE ENGINEER ($$)

Vibrant Primrose Hill pub with garden, ideal after Regent's Park, zoo, or Camden markets.

➕ E2 ✉ 654 Gloucester Avenue, NW1 ☎ 020 7722 0950 🕐 Lunch, dinner
🚇 Camden Town

FIFTH FLOOR AT HARVEY NICHOLS ($$$)

Modern British cuisine for a chic clientele in Julian Wickham's designer room. As an alternative, try the *Fountain* in the basement.

➕ E6 ✉ Knightsbridge, SW1 ☎ 020 7235 5250 🕐 Daily lunch; Mon–Sat dinner
🚇 Knightsbridge

HARRODS ($–$$)

With eateries swinging into action each day, you are spoilt for choice. Favorites include the Champagne and Oyster Bar and the Ice-cream Parlour.

➕ D7 ✉ Knightsbridge, SW1 ☎ 020 7730 1234
🕐 Breakfast, lunch, tea
🚇 Knightsbridge

LAMB TAVERN ($)

Regulars claim this restored Victorian pub in Leadenhall Market serves the best hot roast beef sandwiches in the City.

➕ K5 ✉ 10–12 Leadenhall Market, EC3 ☎ 020 7626 2454
🕐 Mon–Fri lunch 🚇 Bank or Monument

PEASANT ($)

Excellent innovative Italian food in a pub touched with the wand of a design-conscious foodie.

➕ H4 ✉ 240 St. John Street, EC1 ☎ 020 7336 7726
🕐 Mon–Fri lunch; Mon–Sat dinner
🚇 Farringdon

SOTHEBY'S CAFÉ ($$)

The lobby of this auction house is great for a light lunch—reservations are essential—or for a pleasant afternoon tea.

➕ B7 ✉ 34 Bond Street, W1 ☎ 020 7293 5077
🕐 Mon–Fri breakfast, lunch, tea
🚇 Bond Street

MUSEUM RESTAURANTS

Hugely improved, it is now possible to mix quality culture with quality eating at a number of London's museums. Try the Tate Modern (➤ 47), British Museum (➤ 45, 56), National Portrait Gallery (➤ 40), Wallace Collection (➤ 53), Dulwich Picture Gallery (➤ 52), Geffrye Museum (➤ 52), National Gallery (➤ 41), and Somerset House (➤ 43). The Royal Academy's restaurant is decorated by Academicians (➤ 53). Kensington Palace's magnificent Orangery (➤ 27) offers the ultimate tea.

EAT AS MUCH AS YOU CAN BUFFET DEALS

Unlimited food at a fixed price is practical for families with growing children—or simply for hungry adults. Many larger hotels do breakfast and lunch buffets, especially good on Sundays when many Indian restaurants do the same—the Contad Hotel's luxurious buffet is legendary.

Shopping Areas

OPENING TIMES

Regular store hours are 9:30 or 10AM until between 5:30 and 7PM, with late-night shopping in Knightsbridge on Wednesdays and Oxford Street, Regent Street, and Covent Garden on Thursdays.
London's stores tend to be found in clusters; conserve your energy and shop in one area.

TAX-FREE GOODS

If you are a non-E.U. passport holder, consider the VAT Retails Export Scheme. VAT (Value Added Tax) is rated at 17½ percent in Britain and payable on almost everything except books, food, and children's clothes. All non-E.U. passport holders are exempt from VAT if they are taking the goods out of the country within three months. The tax must be paid first, then claimed back. You must have your passport and return ticket with you; the shop assistant will help you complete the form VAT407— make sure you keep your part of it along with the export sales bill. Show Customs this form and have your goods ready to show.

BOND STREET

Bond Street mixes haute couture outlets with art galleries. Asprey & Garrard, one of the world's great luxury stores, is here, as are the Fine Art Society and Sotheby's.
✚ F5 ✉ Mayfair, W1 🚇 Bond Street or Green Park

BROMPTON CROSS

Sophisticated fashion and design stores. The Conran Shop, selling quality design furniture, is the longest-established retailer.
✚ D7 ✉ Knightsbridge/Chelsea, SW3 🚇 Knightsbridge or South Kensington

JERMYN STREET

Once the local street for aristocrats swarming around St. James's Palace; the atmosphere of Jermyn Street remains select: Floris the perfumier (est. 1730); Paxton & Whitfield for cheeses; and Harvie & Hudson or Turnbull & Asser for shirts.
✚ F6 ✉ St. James's, SW1 🚇 Piccadilly Circus or Green Park

KENSINGTON CHURCH STREET

This once-quiet lane now has more than 50 antiques stores, Clarke's restaurant bakery, and Kensington Place.
✚ B6 ✉ Kensington, W8 🚇 Notting Hill Gate or High Street Kensington

NEAL STREET

The epitome of Covent Garden's successful rebirth, this pedestrian street is packed with exotic little stores: Neal Street East, the Kite Store and, in Neal's Yard, a feast of wholefoods.
✚ G5 ✉ Covent Garden, WC2 🚇 Covent Garden

OLD COMPTON STREET

In the 18th century, this was the social center for French exiles. Pâtisserie Valerie at No. 44 (► 69) keeps the mood alive; Italians run the tiny Pollo and Presto bars, Vinorio, Camisa, and the newsstand Moroni's.
✚ F5 ✉ Soho, W1 🚇 Tottenham Court Road

OXFORD STREET

The capital's main shopping artery. At the west end, Marks & Spencer; in the middle the revamped Selfridges & Co, and branches of all significant chains from Body Shop to Gap and John Lewis; at the east end, Tottenham Court Road's electrical and home stores.
✚ E5–G5 ✉ Mayfair/Marylebone, W1 🚇 Oxford Circus, Bond Street, Marble Arch, Tottenham Court Road

REGENT STREET

With its dramatic curve north from Piccadilly, John Nash's street is as smart as intended: Tower Records, Austin Reed, the sumptuous Café Royal, Mappin & Webb (silver), Hamleys (toys ► 60), Liberty (► 73), and the Disney store. North of Oxford Street lies the excellent BBC store.
✚ F5 ✉ Mayfair/Soho, W1 🚇 Piccadilly Circus or Oxford Street

Department Stores

FORTNUM & MASON
Before going in, do not miss the clock, which has Messrs. Fortnum and Mason mincing forward each hour. Prices are high, but the store-brand goods make perfect presents.

✚ F6　✉ 181 Piccadilly, W1
☎ 020 7734 8040
Ⓔ Piccadilly Circus or Green Park

GENERAL TRADING COMPANY
Chic, small-scale department store with quality buys in all areas from china to gardening. Good mail-order catalog.

✚ E7　✉ 144 Sloane Street, SW1　☎ 020 7730 0411
Ⓔ Sloane Square

HARRODS
This vast emporium contains just about everything anyone could want, and 19 places to eat. Apart from the revamped fashion departments, do not miss the spectacular food halls.

✚ D6　✉ Knightsbridge, SW1
☎ 020 7730 1234
Ⓔ Knightsbridge

HARVEY NICHOLS
London's classiest clothes store, from its original storefront window displays to the well-stocked fashion floors. A girl's shopping dream.

✚ E6　✉ 109–25 Knightsbridge, SW1　☎ 020 7235 5000　Ⓔ Knightsbridge

JOHN LEWIS
Its slogan, "never knowingly undersold," inspires a confidence that prices are solidly fair.

✚ F5　✉ Oxford Street, W1
☎ 020 7629 7711　Ⓔ Oxford Circus

LIBERTY
Offering everything from sumptuous fabrics to china and glass, this store's quality is characterized by exoticism and cutting-edge fashion mixed with an Arts and Crafts heritage and a beautiful buiding.

✚ F5　✉ Regent Street, W1
☎ 020 7734 1234　Ⓔ Oxford Circus

MARKS & SPENCER
Most people buy something at M&S. Clothes now have sharper styles, and the food departments offer an exceptional range of pre-prepared meals.

✚ E5　✉ 458 Oxford Street, W1　☎ 020 7935 7954
Ⓔ Marble Arch

SCOTCH HOUSE
Plaid and more plaid on three floors. Especially good for soft lambswool and cashmere woolens, as well as traditional, quality Scottish clothing.

✚ D6　✉ 2 Brompton Road, SW1　☎ 020 7581 2151
Ⓔ South Kensington

SELFRIDGES & CO
Less glitzy than Harrods, but equally good for the whole family. This vast, bedazzling store stocks beauty products, designer labels, china, glass, and electrical goods. The food hall is worth exploring. Christmas window displays are usually wonderful.

✚ E5　✉ 400 Oxford Street, W1　☎ 020 7629 1234
Ⓔ Marble Arch or Bond Street

ONE-STOP SHOPPING

The one-stop shopping that department stores offer has several advantages over schlepping around the streets. If it rains, you stay dry. If you are hungry, there are cafés. There are also the services to be considered. Your purchases from various departments can be held for you while you shop, to be collected together at the end. Garments can be altered, presents wrapped, and writing paper printed. And most stores have dependable after-sales service if something is not right.

Street Markets

FASHION

To buy international high fashion, explore Harvey Nichols (► 73) and the stores lining Knightsbridge, Sloane Street, Brompton Cross, Beauchamp Place, Bond Street, South Molton Street, and St. Christopher's Place. For more dramatic, innovative, streetwise fashion, explore Urban Outfitters (on ✉ Kensington High Street, W8), then visit Vivienne Westwood (✉ 6 Davies Street, W1), American Retro (✉ 35 Old Compton Street, W1) and, in Covent Garden, florence-b (✉ 37 Neal Street, WC2), Monsoon (✉ 6 Davies Street, W1 and branches), Carharrt (✉ 56 Neal Street, WC2), Diesel (✉ 43 Earlham Gardens, WC2), and Duffer of St. George (✉ 29 Shorts Gardens, WC2).

SMITHFIELD MEAT MARKET

Smithfields (EC1) is the only large, fresh-food, commercial market left in central London. Thousands of bloody carcasses hung up on iron hooks are traded in Horace Jones's grand 19th-century building. Trading starts at 5AM and the market closes down at noon (Mon–Fri).

BERMONDSEY (NEW CALEDONIAN MARKET)

You need to know your stuff here—and, as the big dealers and auction-house experts get here before dawn, the earlier you go the better.

✚ L7 ✉ Long Lane and Bermondsey Street, SE1 🕐 Fri 5–2 🚇 Borough or London Bridge

BRIXTON MARKET

Best to go on Saturday, when the streets buzz with local African and Caribbean community shoppers buying their mangoes, sweet potatoes, snapper fish, calf's feet, and ready-cooked delicacies.

✚ Off map at H10 ✉ Brixton Station Road, Electric Avenue, and Popes Road, SW9 🕐 Mon, Tue, Thu–Sat 8–6; Wed 8–3 🚇 Brixton 🚉 Brixton

CAMDEN MARKETS

The small, vibrant market in Camden Lock has expanded and spawned other markets to fill every patch of space from the underground station up to Hawley Road. Find crafts, clothes, books, and more.

✚ E2 ✉ Camden High Street to Chalk Farm Road, NW1 🕐 all markets Sat–Sun; some open other days, too 🚇 Camden Town

CAMDEN PASSAGE

Bargain at the large, twice-weekly open-air antiques market held in front of the antiques stores; then try Chapel Street market across Upper Street.

✚ H3 ✉ Islington, N1 🕐 Wed 9–mid-afternoon; Sat 9–5 🚇 Angel

GREENWICH MARKET

Hundreds of stands selling antiques and crafts, clothes, old books, and more. A good start to a Greenwich day (► 20).

✉ College Approach, Stockwell Street and corner of High Road and Royal Hill, SE10 🕐 Sat, Sun 9–6 🚉 Cutty Sark or Island Gardens DLR then walk through the tunnel

LEADENHALL MARKET

A surprising City treat housed under Horace Jones's 1880s arcades, with quality butchers, cheesemongers, fish-mongers, and pubs.

✚ K5 ✉ Leadenhall, EC3 🕐 Mon–Fri 8–4 🚇 Bank or Monument

PETTICOAT LANE MARKET

Originally a Tudor clothes market; Jewish immigration stimulated its growth into Victorian London's largest market. Bargain hard for fashion, leather, household goods, and knickknacks. Brick Lane market is nearby.

✚ K5 ✉ Middlesex Street, E1 🕐 Sun 9–2 🚇 Aldgate or Aldgate East

PORTOBELLO MARKET

Saturday is the big day, when antiques and not-so-antiques are sold from the stores and the solid line of vendors in front of them. There are lower prices further down the hill, with secondhand stands beneath Westway.

✚ B5 ✉ Portobello Road, W11 🕐 Fruit and vegetables Mon–Sat. General Fri 8–3. Antiques Sat 6–6 🚇 Ladbroke Grove

Art & Antiques

ANTIQUARIUS

London's oldest antiques center houses 120 dealers whose goods include lace, old clothes, and jewelry; there are plenty of quirky, affordable items here.

🔠 D8 ✉ 131–41 King's Road, SW3 ☎ 020 7351 5353
🚇 Sloane Square

BONHAM'S

The strength of this auction house lies in its 20th-century and specialist sales. Less expensive goods are sold in its Chelsea Galleries.

🔠 D7 ✉ Montpelier Galleries, Montpelier Street, SW7 ☎ 020 7393 3900 🚇 Knightsbridge

CHRISTIE'S

The auction house has departments ranging from grand old masters to coins and tribal art. A second, less expensive sale room is in South Kensington.

🔠 F6 ✉ Christie's International Ltd., 8 King Street, SW1 ☎ 020 7839 9060
🚇 Green Park

THE FINE ART SOCIETY

One of the oldest and friendliest galleries in town.

🔠 F5 ✉ 148 New Bond Street, W1 ☎ 020 7629 5116
🚇 Bond Street

GRAY'S ANTIQUE MARKET

High-quality goods ranging from pictures to silver are sold at 170 stands.

🔠 E5 ✉ 1–7 Davies Mews and 58 Davies Street, W1 ☎ 020 7629 7034
🚇 Bond Street

LOTS ROAD CHELSEA AUCTION GALLERIES

Eclectic mix of antique, reproduction, and good contemporary designer furniture.

🔠 C9 ✉ 71–4 Lots Road, SW10 ☎ 020 7351 7771
🚇 Sloane Square then it's a 20-minute walk or bus No. 19 or 22

SOTHEBY'S

The world's largest auction house. This is a rabbit warren of sale rooms with objects of all kinds on display. The "Colonnade" sales are less expensive.

🔠 F5 ✉ 34 New Bond Street, W1 ☎ 020 7293 5000
🚇 Bond Street

SPINK-LEGER PICTURES

Top English paintings by artists such as Turner and Gainsborough; Agnew's, Colnaghi, Frost & Reed, Fine Art Society, and Philip Mould nearby are also worth visiting.

🔠 F6 ✉ 13 Old Bond Street, W1 ☎ 020 7629 3538
🚇 Green Park

SPINK & SON

Best known for their coins, medals, stamps, and banknotes.

🔠 G4 ✉ 69 Southampton Row, WC1 ☎ 020 7563 4000
🚇 Holborn

WADDINGTON GALLERIES

In a small street lined with about 20 galleries selling modern art, Waddington is just one worth seeing; try also Theo Waddington, Redfern, and Browse & Darby. Also worth exploring are Clifford and Derring Streets nearby.

🔠 F5 ✉ 11 Cork Street, W1 ☎ 020 7851 2200
🚇 Green Park

BUYING AT AUCTION

Watching an auction is one thing; buying is quite another. At the pre-sale viewing, inspect any lot you may bid for and check its description and estimated sale price in the catalog. If you cannot attend the sale, leave a bid; if you can, decide on your maximum bid and do not go above it! Bid by lifting your hand up high. If successful, pay and collect after the sale, or arrange for delivery.

PRIVATE GALLERIES

An indispensible tool for visitors getting to grips with commercial art galleries in London is the monthly *Galleries* magazine, available free from most galleries. With its maps and specialist subject index, information can be called up by area as well as subject.

Books, New & Old

BOOKSTORES & CAFÉS

To browse in a bookstore with its own in-house café, try Borders Books, Music and Cafe (🎧 203 Oxford Street, W1 ☎ 020 7292 1600 🚇 Mon–Sat 8AM–11PM, Sun noon–6 🚇 Oxford Circus); their Charing Cross Road branch also has a café. Central London branches of Books Etc with cafés include those on Charing Cross Road, Oxford Street, and Piccadilly. Waterstone's superstore on Piccadilly has a café, juice bar, and restaurant.

ELECTRONIC BARGAINS

To Europeans, London prices for electrical goods seem good value; to Americans they seem expensive. If you know what you want, compare prices up and down Tottenham Court Road for stereos, and look there as well as New Oxford Street for computers. Micro Anvika, on Tottenham Court Road, is good for hardware, software, and CD-ROMs. If daunted, go to John Lewis, Selfridges, or Harrods (► 73); all have good after sales service.

BERNARD QUARITCH

It is best to make an appointment to come to this, the most splendid and serious of the city's antiquarian bookstores.
➕ F5 ✉ 5 Lower John Street, W1 ☎ 020 7734 2983 🚇 Piccadilly Circus

BOOKS FOR COOKS

Possibly the world's best selection of books about cooking and cuisine; orders are taken and dispatched worldwide.
➕ A5 ✉ 4 Blenheim Crescent, W11 ☎ 020 7221 1992 🚇 Ladbroke Grove

CINEMA BOOKSHOP

London's greatest selection of books on the movies ever. Well–informed staff, plus mail order.
➕ G5 ✉ 13–14 Great Russell Street, WC1 ☎ 020 7637 0206 🚇 Tottenham Court Road

DAUNT BOOKS

In his paneled and stained-glass elegant 1910 shop, James Daunt keeps an impressive stock of travelogs and guides.
➕ E4 ✉ 83 Marylebone High Street, NW1 ☎ 020 7224 2295 🚇 Baker Street

EDWARD STANFORD

London's largest selection of maps of countries, cities, and even very small towns around the world, together with travel books.
➕ G5 ✉ 12–14 Long Acre, WC2 ☎ 020 7836 1321 🚇 Covent Garden

FORBIDDEN PLANET

An amazing selection of fantasy, horror, science fiction; plus comic books.
➕ G5 ✉ 71–3 New Oxford Street, W1 ☎ 020 7836 4179 🚇 Tottenham Court Road

HATCHARDS

Opened in 1797; past patrons have included British army commander, the Duke of Wellington (1769–1852) and four-time prime minister William Gladstone (1809–98). With their well-informed staff, Hatchards still knows how to make book buying a delicious experience.
➕ F6 ✉ 187 Piccadilly, W1 ☎ 020 7493 9921 🚇 Piccadilly Circus

MAGGS BROTHERS

Make your appointment, then step into this Mayfair mansion to find an out-of-print book, a first edition, or rare antiquarian book.
➕ E6 ✉ 50 Berkeley Square, W1 ☎ 020 7493 7160 🚇 Green Park

WATERSTONE'S

Europe's largest bookstore stocks more than 250,000 titles and has a restaurant, café, and Internet area.
➕ F6 ✉ 203–6 Piccadilly, W1 ☎ 020 7851 2400 🚇 Piccadilly Circus

ZWEMMER ARTS BOOKSHOP

Art books fill three neighboring bookstores, divided by category. Here, fine art is upstairs, decorative art and architecture downstairs. Photography and media at 80 Charing Cross Road; Graphic Design at 72 Charing Cross Road.
➕ G5 ✉ 24 Litchfield Street, WC2 ☎ 020 7240 4158 🚇 Leicester Square

China & Glass

ARAM DESIGNS LTD

Aram's international modern design includes works by Depadova.

🕂 G5 ✉ 3 Kean Street, WC2 ☎ 020 7240 3933 Ⓔ Aldwych or Covent Garden

ARIA

Aria stocks modern international state-of-the-art design, with plenty of Italian pieces on display. There is a second shop across the road devoted to bathroom accessories.

🕂 H2 ✉ 133 Upper Street, N1 ☎ 020 7226 1021 Ⓔ Angel

CERAMICA BLUE

Huge collection of functional and decorative contemporary ceramic designs, made exclusively by potters from all over the world.

🕂 A5 ✉ 10 Blenheim Crescent, W11 ☎ 020 7727 0288 Ⓔ Ladbroke Grove

DESIGNER'S GUILD

Tricia Guild's store is a wonderland of exquisite design. Contemporary china, glass, and irresistible fabrics.

🕂 D8 ✉ 277 King's Road, SW3 ☎ 020 7351 5775 Ⓔ Sloane Square then 15 minutes' walk or bus 19 or 22

HEAL'S

A frontrunner of the Arts and Crafts movement in the 1920s, Heal's specializes in timeless contemporary furniture.

🕂 F4 ✉ 196 Tottenham Court Road, W1 ☎ 020 7636 1666 Ⓔ Goodge Street

INFINITY

Some of the best modern glassware in town, specializing in wine glasses, goblets, fruit bowls, and vases; colors are jewel-like.

🕂 G5 ✉ 8 Upper St Martin's Lane, WC2 ☎ 020 7497 1011 Ⓔ Leicester Square

JEANETTE HAYHURST

One of the few places to find old glass, especially British pieces. Also stocks interesting studio glass.

🕂 B6 ✉ 32a Kensington Church Street, W8 ☎ 020 7938 1539 Ⓔ High Street Kensington

PURVES & PURVES

Alessi, Starck, and a host of contemporary designers.

🕂 F4 ✉ Tottenham Court Road, W1 ☎ 020 7580 8223 Ⓔ Goodge Street

THOMAS GOODE & CO

Collectors of Meissen and Dresden need look no further than this splendid showroom. Also stockists of Lalique and Baccarat crystal.

🕂 E6 ✉ 19 South Audley Street, W1 ☎ 020 7499 2823 Ⓔ Green Park

WATERFORD WEDGWOOD

The largest selection of handmade, full lead crystal Waterford glass—all made in Ireland—and Wedgwood china. Will phone the factory for special orders, help customers search for designs no longer made, and ship goods worldwide.

🕂 F5 ✉ 173–4 Piccadilly, W1 ☎ 020 7629 2614 Ⓔ Piccadilly Circus

Do not worry about breaking your valuable purchases on the way home; they can be packed and sent there for you, fully insured.

SILVER

English silver is one of the best antiques buys because it has been hallmarked since the mid-17th century, so you know precisely what you are buying. To get a good look, wander the London Silver Vaults on Chancery Lane, Antiquarius (► 75), Gray's Antique Market (► 75), Asprey's on Bond Street, Garrard, and Mappin & Webb on Regent Street (► 72). Buy at these locations or visit Christine Schell (✉ 15 Cale Street, SW3) for silver and tortoiseshell, or John Jesse (✉ 160 Kensington Church Street, W8) for art deco.

Museum & Gallery Shops

SPECIALTY SHOPS

Specialty shops come in every shape and size. Stanley Gibbons (✉ 399 Strand, WC2) is a philatelist's paradise, while James Smith & Sons (✉ 53 New Oxford Street, W1) stocks every kind of umbrella to keep British rain at bay. Other favorites include Christopher Farr (✉ 115 Regent's Park Road, NW1) for contemporary carpets, the Crafts Council Shop (✉ 44 Pentonville Road, N1 and at the V&A ➤ 30), Paperchase (✉ 213 Tottenham Court Road, W1) and Smythson's (✉ 44 New Bond Street, W1), both stationers. BBC World Service Shop (✉ Bush House, Strand, WC2) and the BBC Shop (✉ Regent Street, W1) stock videos, cassettes, and books related to their programs; ideal for presents.

To find the specialty shop you want, use the Yellow Pages telephone directory, which is listed by subject.

BRITISH LIBRARY
(➤ 56)
Plenty of books, but other collection-inspired objects, too.

BRITISH MUSEUM
(➤ 45)
Books, games, and design objects. Especially strong on Egypt-influenced goods.

DESIGN MUSEUM
(➤ 52)
Extensive and immensely chic designer goods, some with high price tags.

LONDON AQUARIUM
(➤ 53)
The world beneath the seas packaged to delight and educate.

MUSEUM OF LONDON
(➤ 49)
Good for souvenirs and books about London.

NATIONAL GALLERY
(➤ 41)
Two large shops; particularly good for paper goods and diaries.

NATIONAL PORTRAIT GALLERY (➤ 40)
Surprisingly large store, well stocked with books on historical figures and British history; own-brand children's book projects.

NATURAL HISTORY MUSEUM (➤ 28)
Thousands of dinosaurs to read about, cut out, or put on the mantelpiece; plus plenty about the world since then. Excellent separate bookstores covering every aspect of natural history conceivable for adults and children.

QUEEN'S GALLERY & ROYAL MEWS (➤ 34)
The largest selection of publications and memorabilia about the British royal family.

ROYAL ACADEMY
(➤ 53)
If you cannot own a work by a Royal Academician, then buy a plate, mug, pen, or book specially designed by one for the RA store.

ROYAL BOTANICAL GARDENS, KEW (➤ 26)
Comprehensive selection of goods and publications—many lavishly illustrated to keep the most ardent gardener happy.

SCIENCE MUSEUM
(➤ 29)
Plenty of books and projects for budding scientists of all ages.

TATE GALLERIES
(➤ 36, 47)
The annual Tate diary, its pages scattered with reproductions from the Modern and British collections, is a collector's item; also an extensive collection of quality posters.

VICTORIA & ALBERT MUSEUM (➤ 30)
You could do a full-scale Christmas shop here, from toys and books to unique crafts. Many collection-inspired goods.

Food & Wine

BERRY BROS & RUDD

Opened as a grocery store in 1699; the wines range from popular varieties to specialty madeiras, ports, and clarets. Their own-label bottles are also good value. Perfect service.

🏠 F6 ✉ 3 St. James's Street, SW1 ☎ 020 7396 9600 Ⓖ Green Park

THE BLOOMSBURY WINE AND SPIRIT COMPANY

In addition to wines, the strength of this store is its Scottish malt whiskeys: more than 170 in stock.

🏠 G4 ✉ 3 Bloomsbury Street, WC1 ☎ 020 7436 4763/4 Ⓖ Tottenham Court Road

CARLUCCIO'S

A designer deli stocking only the most refined goods, such as truffle oil, black pasta, and balsamic vinegar.

🏠 G5 ✉ 30 Neal Street, WC2 ☎ 020 7240 1487 Ⓖ Covent Garden

FRESH & WILD

Glorious organic foods, plus ready-to-eat preparations and a juice bar. Five other London branches.

🏠 F2 ✉ 49 Parkway Crescent, NW1 ☎ 020 7428 7575 Ⓖ Camden Town

NEAL'S YARD DAIRY

A temple to the British cheese, where more than 50 varieties from small farms in Britain are ripened to perfection.

🏠 G5 ✉ 17 Shorts Gardens, WC2 ☎ 020 7240 5700 Ⓖ Covent Garden

ODDBINS

With more than 60 branches in London, Oddbins is strong on quality, range, and price.

🏠 G5 ✉ 23 Earlham Street, WC2 ☎ 020 7836 6331 Ⓖ Covent Garden

ROCOCO

Delicious, imaginative chocolates—go for artisan bars flavored with Earl Grey tea, chili pepper, nutmeg, cardamom, or wild mint leaves.

🏠 D8 ✉ 321 King's Road, SW3 ☎ 020 7352 5857 Ⓖ Sloane Square

R TWINING & CO

The little, atmospheric shop where the tea merchant set up his business in 1706.

🏠 H5 ✉ 216 Strand, WC2 ☎ 020 7353 3511 Ⓖ Temple

TOM'S

Basement deli sells breads, patisserie, cheeses, cold meats, preserved lemons, olives, and caviar. Bustling café on the first floor.

🏠 B5 ✉ 226 Westbourne Grove, W11 ☎ 020 7221 8818 Ⓖ Bayswater

VILLANDRY

Quality "foodstore" with best buys taking in French and English cheeses, great breads, olive oil, and much more.

🏠 F5 ✉ 170 Great Portland Street, W1N ☎ 020 7631 3131 Ⓖ Great Portland Street

VINOPOLIS

Mouthwatering breads, cheese, olives, and of course, wines in a shop adjoining the wine tour (➤ 62).

🏠 J6 ✉ Bank End, SE1 ☎ 0870 4444 777 Ⓖ London Bridge

WINE

London has an unrivaled variety of international wines at the best prices, for, although Britain is not a major wine-producing country, the British like to drink wine and know about it. This explains the range, quality, and fiercely competitive prices in the chains (Oddbins, Threshers) and the supermarkets (Sainsbury's, Safeway, Waitrose, and Tesco). For bulk buying, consider the Majestic Warehouse chain, a reliable wine merchant, or Christie's and Sotheby's regular wine auctions (➤ 75).

MAKE A PICNIC

With so many parks and benches to choose from in London, a picnic makes a good break from a hard morning's sightseeing or shopping. The big stores have some of the most seductive food halls—and they stock wine; see Harrods, Selfridges, Fortnum & Mason, and Marks & Spencer (all ➤ 73). Old Compton Street (➤ 72) is a food shopper's delight; see also Clarke's Bakery (✉ 122 Kensington Church Street, W8) and other cafés that sell their own prepared food to take-out.

Theater

THEATER TIPS

If you care about where you sit, go in person and peruse the plan. For an evening "Sold out" performance, it is worth lining up for returns; otherwise, try for a matinee. The most inexpensive seats could be far from the stage or uncomfortable, so take binoculars and a cushion. As for dress, Londoners rarely dress up for the theater anymore; but they do order their intermission drinks before the play starts, and remain seated while they applaud.

TICKET–BUYING TIPS

Use the tkts Half-price Ticket Booth (see this page). Preview tickets are lower in price, as are matinée tickets. Get up early and line up for one-day bargain tickets at the RNT and RSC. Go with friends and make a party booking at a reduced rate. Ask the National Theatre, RSC, Royal Court, and other theaters about special discounts on particular performances; and keep student and senior citizen cards ready. Remember, the show is the same wherever you sit!

INFORMATION

Theater in London covers a wide range of venues. It is vibrant, varied, and extensive. *Time Out*, London's weekly entertainment guide, provides an exhaustive list of all theaters, plus reviews. Daily newspapers carry a less complete but totally up-to-date listing, with more reviews. Ticket prices are lowest for fringe, more expensive for West End, and very expensive for musicals.

TICKET BUYING

Telephone booking can be done using a credit card, which must be produced when collecting the tickets. If you book without a credit card, you must usually arrive at the theater 40 minutes before curtain-up—or else the tickets will be put back for sale. Booking in person means you can see the seating plan—a good idea if you want a decent seat in some of London's older theaters. Ask for information on leg room and sight lines.

TICKET AGENCIES

Ticketmaster ☎ 020 7344 4444 and First Call ☎ 020 7420 0000 are both reliable. West End Cares ☎ 020 7413 1142 is a charity hot line with a donation to AIDS charities included in the price. Some shows have no booking fee, others a small one, and a few rise to 22 percent of the ticket price, so ask first. Beware: it is unwise to buy from small agencies, and very unwise to buy from scalpers.

TKTS

Each day a limited number of tickets for some West End shows is sold for that day's performance at half price, plus a £2 service charge. The rules are: a maximum of four tickets per person, no exchanges or returns. ✚ G5 ✉ Leicester Square, WC2 ⊙ Mon–Sat 10–7; Sun noon–3:30 ⊕ Leicester Square or Piccadilly Circus

THE THEATER YEAR

The theaters are never dark. At any one time there will be an average of 45 West End theaters playing a range of musicals, drama, comedy, and thrillers, as well as staging opera and dance. LIFT (London International Festival of Theatre) spreads its festival night around the year, staging exciting productions in unusual venues. The Royal Shakespeare Company (RSC) holds an annual festival, often at the Almeida or Young Vic theaters.

WEST END THEATERS

The Society of London Theatres (SOLT) represents the owners, managers, and producers of 54 major London theaters. SOLT runs the annual Laurence Olivier Awards—London's answer to the Tonys—publishes the fortnightly London Theatre Guide (free from theaters), and runs a Theatre Token scheme ☎ 020 7240 8800 and the tkts Half-price Ticket Booth (see above).

ROYAL NATIONAL THEATRE (RNT)

British and world drama, classics and new plays. Home of the National Theatre company, it has three performance spaces—the Olivier, the Lyttelton, and the Cottesloe. All have several productions in repertory.

H6 ✉ South Bank, SE1 ☎ Information and tours 020 7452 3400. Theater tickets 020 7452 3000 🚇 Embankment or Waterloo 🚃 Waterloo

ROYAL SHAKESPEARE THEATRE (RSC)

The London home of the Royal Shakespeare Company, who perform in season in the Barbican Theatre (level 3) and The Pit (level 1). Some productions are new, others are from Stratford; several productions may be running concurrently in repertory. There is an annual Prom season, plus backstage tours.

J4 ✉ Barbican Centre, Silk Street, EC2 ☎ 020 7638 8891. Range of good ticket deals 🚇 Barbican

MUSICALS

The successful, long-running shows are dominated by the great impresarios. Sir Andrew Lloyd Webber, who restored and owns the Palace Theatre, has staged *Starlight Express*, *Sunset Boulevard*, *Phantom of the Opera*, and *Cats*, the latter two with Cameron Mackintosh, who has had great success with the adaptation of Victor Hugo's novel of the French Revolution, *Les Misérables*.

LONG-RUNNING STALWARTS

Few plays have the sustained, long-running success of the musicals. Most famous is Agatha Christie's *The Mousetrap* at St. Martin's, aiming for its 50th anniversary in 2002. At the Fortune Theatre, *The Woman in Black* began its run in 1989.

OFF–WEST END THEATER

This new category honors the fringe theaters that still stage imaginative productions. Look in the listings for the Almeida, the Bush, Donmar Warehouse, Drill Hall, the Gate, Hampstead, ICA, King's Head, Lyric Studio, Riverside Studios, Royal Court, Theatre Royal Stratford East, Tricycle, and the Young Vic.

FRINGE AND PUB THEATER

True fringe, or "alternative" theater in London is vibrant, varied, and dotted about in over 35 venues, many of them pubs. Try Etcetera Theatre (at the Oxford Arms pub), Finborough, the Hen & Chickens, Man in the Moon, New End Theatre, Old Red Lion, and the White Bear.

COMEDY

The Comedy Store is hugely popular. Also try the Banana Cabaret, Jongleurs at the Cornet, Comedy Café, Red Rose Comedy Store, and Meccano Club, a restored music hall that holds vaudeville nights.

OPEN-AIR THEATER

If the weather is good, grab a picnic and head for the Open Air Theatre, Regent's Park (Jun–Sep), Greenwich Old Observatory (Jul–Aug), or Holland Park Theatre (Jun–Aug).

CHILDREN'S THEATER

Several theaters stage magical performances all year around. Names to look for include the Little Angel Marionette Theatre (doyen of puppet theaters), Polka Children's Theatre, and the Unicorn Theatre for Children. Ask about children's productions at the National and the RSC, as well as Punch and Judy shows in Covent Garden Piazza.

REVIVED THEATERS

Some old London theaters have been revived. Andrew Lloyd Webber restored his 1880s Cambridge Theatre. The Theatre Royal, Haymarket, has new gold leaf, while the Savoy and the Criterion have been meticulously restored. Out of the West End, the Richmond Theatre has reopened. On the south bank, there is the splendidly ornate Old Vic Theatre and the small-scale Globe theater opened in 1997, designed in the manner of Burbage's original where Shakespeare worked.

Classical Music, Opera & Ballet

FOOD WITH MUSIC

For starters, there are tea dances at Le Meridien Waldorf. Claridges' cocktails with their Hungarian Quartet are an institution, while a dinner dance at the Savoy, Ritz, and Claridges is opulently romantic (► 86).
Blues (✉ 42 Dean Street, W1), Café Boheme (✉ 13 Old Compton Street, W1), Ketteners (✉ 29 Romilly Street, W1), and Pizza Pomodoro (✉ 51 Beauchamp Place, SW3 and branches) are altogether more informal.

MUSIC EVERYWHERE!

London is full of music. At lunchtime, the best places are churches, where the regular concerts are usually free. Look in *Time Out* listings (► 80) for: St. Anne, St. Agnes, and St. Olave's in the City; St. James's, Piccadilly, in the West End. St. Paul's Cathedral evensong is mid-afternoon. On Sundays, cathedrals and churches are again best for sacred music. Look for concerts in historic houses, museums, and galleries, especially during the City of London Festival (July). Finally, music is played outdoors in the royal parks, Embankment Gardens, and elsewhere, but best of all at Kenwood (► 31) or Marble Hill, Richmond, on summer evenings.

THE MUSIC YEAR

Runs non stop. Look for festivals such as the City of London, Spitalfields, Almeida, and Hampton Court Palace, and traditions such as the Christmas Oratorios, carol singing in Trafalgar Square, and the Easter Passions. The major classic festival is the Proms, a nickname for the Henry Wood Promenade Concerts, held daily at the Royal Albert Hall and elsewhere from mid-July to mid-September, and broadcast live on BBC Radio 3.

THE DANCE YEAR

Very lively, with great variety. Highpoints include the Coliseum's summer season, the Royal Ballet's performances at the Royal Opera House, and the Nutcracker Suite season at the Royal Festival Hall (Dec–Jan). Other major venues are: Sadler's Wells, the Place, ICA, and Riverside Studios. The climax of the year is Dance Umbrella, a world showcase for contemporary dance (Oct–Nov).

THE OPERA YEAR

Grand opera alternates with dance at the Royal Opera House. Cheaper and often more vibrant opera takes place at the larger Coliseum (performances in English). In addition, there are visits from Welsh National Opera, Opera North, and Opera Factory, and open-air opera performances in Holland Park and by Kenwood Lake.

MAJOR VENUES

BARBICAN CONCERT HALL
✚ J4 ✉ Barbican Centre, Silk Street, EC2 ☎ 020 7638 4141. Reservations 020 7638 8891. Credit card reservations 020 7638 8891, daily 9–8. Range of good ticket deals ⊜ Barbican

LONDON COLISEUM
✚ G5 ✉ St. Martin's Lane, WC2 ☎ 020 7632 8300 ⊜ Leicester Square

ROYAL ALBERT HALL
✚ C6 ✉ Kensington Gore, SW7 ☎ 020 7589 3203. Reservations 020 7589 8212 ⊜ South Kensington

ROYAL OPERA HOUSE
Finally reopened in December 1999 after major refurbishment, this is the venue for opera and the home of the Royal Ballet.
✚ G5 ✉ Covent Garden, WC2 ☎ 020 7304 4000 ⊜ Covent Garden

SADLER'S WELLS THEATRE
The most electrifying dance theater in Europe, newly built for 2000—a must for all ballet fans.
✚ H3 ✉ Rosebery Avenue, EC1 ☎ 020 7863 8000 ⊜ Angel

SOUTH BANK
Royal Festival Hall, Queen Elizabeth Hall, and Purcell Room.
✚ G6–H6 ✉ South Bank, SE1 ☎ 020 7960 4242 ⊜ Waterloo

WIGMORE HALL
✚ E5 ✉ 36 Wigmore Street, W1 ☎ 020 7935 2141 ⊜ Bond Street

Jazz & Pub Music

THE AVENUE

A sleek minimalist setting for an upbeat Sunday brunch, served to the cool sounds of a jazz singer with pianist backing.
✚ F5 ✉ 7–9 St. James's Street, SW1 ☎ 020 7321 2111
🚇 Green Park

BULL'S HEAD, BARNES

Seductive combination of good jazz in the friendly village atmosphere of a riverside pub.
✚ Off map at A10 ✉ 373 Lonsdale Road, SW13 ☎ 020 8876 5241 🚉 Barnes Bridge

DOVER STREET

Large, candle-lit, popular basement where the music can be jump jive, jazz, rhythm and blues, or Big Band. The food is good.
✚ F6 ✉ 8–9 Dover Street, W1 ☎ 020 7629 9813
🚇 Piccadilly Circus

HALF MOON PUTNEY

Jolly pub for rhythm and blues played by lesser stars; plenty of audience participation.
✚ Off map at A10 ✉ 93 Lower Richmond Road, SW15 ☎ 020 8780 9383

HOPE & ANCHOR

Tiny pub featuring bands just burgeoning on the scene.
✚ H2 ✉ 207 Upper Street, N1 ☎ 020 7354 1312
🚇 Highbury & Islington
🚉 Highbury & Islington

JAZZ CAFÉ

Current favorite among the young; buzzes nightly with the widest range of jazz, from soul to rap.
✚ F2 ✉ 5 Parkway, NW1 ☎ 020 8963 0940/7344 0044
🚇 Camden Town

MONARCH

Come and hear the Barfly's Club indie music in this Camden pub.
✚ E2 ✉ 49 Chalk Farm Road, NW1 ☎ 020 7691 4244
🚇 Chalk Farm

PIZZA EXPRESS, SOHO

Quality pizzas and great, often mainstream, jazz in this friendly Soho cellar. Several other branches of Pizza Express have live jazz, too.
✚ F5 ✉ 10 Dean Street, W1 ☎ 020 7439 8722
🚇 Tottenham Court Road

PIZZA ON THE PARK

More upscale than its sister, Pizza Express; top foreign names play at one or other venue.
✚ E6 ✉ 11 Knightsbridge, SW1 ☎ 020 7235 5273
🚇 Hyde Park Corner

RONNIE SCOTT'S

One of the world's best-known and most loved jazz clubs, run by jazz musicians for jazz lovers.
✚ F5 ✉ 47 Frith Street, W1 ☎ 020 7439 0747
🚇 Tottenham Court Road

VORTEX

A bit further out but this friendly jazz haunt is worth the trip for its good music and the great, mainly vegetarian food.
✚ Off map at K1 ✉ 139–141 Stoke Newington Church Street, N16 ☎ 020 7254 6516
🚇 Stoke Newington

606 CLUB

Find local and young jazz musicians in the Chelsea border haunt.
✚ C9 ✉ 90 Lots Road, SW10 ☎ 020 7352 5953 🚇 Fulham Broadway

ALL THAT JAZZ

London boasts a great concentration of world-class jazz musicians, both homegrown and foreign, traditional and contemporary—look out for Camden Jazz Week, Capital Jazz Festival, and the Bracknell Festival. Evening and late-night gigs cover rock, roots, rhythm and blues, and more, many in pubs. For a list of venues, check *Time Out*.

PUB MUSIC

This can be one of the least expensive and most enjoyable evenings out in London, worth the trip to an off-beat location. For the price of a pint of beer (usually a huge choice) you can settle down to enjoy the ambience and listen to some of the best alternative music available in town—from folk, jazz, and blues to rhythm and blues, soul, and more. Audiences tend to be friendly, loyal to their venue, and happy to talk music.

Movies & Clubs

London lacks the range of movie theaters to be found in some other cities and often receives foreign films long after their home release. But there is plenty of independent and late-night cinema, making a good beginning to a night of clubbing. Some movie theater seats are half price on Mondays.

One-night clubbing is strong. To find the right club night and club style, consult *Time Out*'s night-by-night listing (► 80) or see the advertisements at regular venues. Dress streetwise and pay at the door.

COCKTAILS AND BARS

For fashionable club-bars try AKA (✉ 18 West Central Street, WC2), Fluid (✉ 40 Charterhouse Street, WEC1), Pop (✉ 14 Soho Street, W1), or Dogstar (✉ 389 Coldharbour Lane, SW9). For pampering cocktails, head for the Savoy's Thames Foyer and Claridge's lounge (► 86). For New York style try the Savoy's American Bar (► 86); this and the Meridien Waldorf's atmospheric bar are ideal pre- or post-theater. To be seen, go to the Dorchester (✉ Park Lane, W1). To be discreet, go to the Connaught (✉ 16 Carlos Place, W1).

MOVIE THEATERS

THE BIG SCREENS
The places to see premiers and commercial first runs. Biggest are the Empire (Cinema 1) and Odeon on Leicester Square, and the ABC on Shaftesbury Avenue.

IMAX CINEMAS (► 61)
For a truly spectacular wraparound cinematic experience.

THE INDEPENDENTS
Show mainstream blockbusters, foreign (subtitled), and offbeat British movies. The most sumptuous are Minema, Lumière, Curzon Mayfair, Barbican, and the Chelsea Cinema; others include the Screen chain, Camden Plaza, Gate, Metro, and Renoir.

NATIONAL FILM THEATRE
Advantages of its two screens: good programming, silent audiences, movie-specialist bookstore, riverside restaurant, children's screenings.
🚇 H6 ✉ South Bank, SE1
☎ 020 7928 3232
Ⓜ Waterloo

REPERTORY
Good for old movies, seasons, double-bills, and late nights. Try the Everyman and the Phoenix; knife-edge contemporary at ICA Cinémathèque; variety at the French and Goethe Institutes. Also go to the Museum of London's "Made in London" series (► 49).

CLUB VENUES

DOGSTAR
Crowded and popular Brixton venue.
🚇 Off the map from H10
✉ 389 Coldharbour Lane, SW9
☎ 020 7733 7515 Ⓜ Brixton

THE END
Varied music in a well-designed West End club.
🚇 G5 ✉ 18 West Central Street, WC1 ☎ 020 7419 9199
Ⓜ Holborn

FABRIC
Dance and hang out with up to 2,500 others at this Clerkenwell super-club.
🚇 H4 ✉ 77A Charterhouse Street, EC1 ☎ 020 7336 8898
Ⓜ Leicester Square

GLASSHOUSE
Three rooms, each with their own music booming.
🚇 J5 ✉ The Mermaid Building, Puddle Dock, off Upper Thames Street, EC4 ☎ 020 7680 0415 Ⓜ Blackfriars

MINISTRY OF SOUND
Glamorous and justly popular, this prison-like building is London's best-known club.
🚇 J7 ✉ 103 Gaunt Street, SE1 ☎ 020 7378 6528
Ⓜ Elephant & Castle

OCEAN
Hackney's super-tech music venue, opened in 2001.
🚇 M2 ✉ 270 Mare Street, E8
☎ 020 8533 0111
Ⓜ Hackney Central

SCALA
Hip hop, breakbeat, and indie in this super-club.
🚇 G3 ✉ King's Cross, N1
☎ 020 7833 2022
Ⓜ King's Cross

Spectator Sports

THE MAJOR VENUES

ALL ENGLAND LAWN TENNIS CHAMPIONSHIPS, WIMBLEDON

Tennis's top tournament starts late June. Enter the ticket ballot or join lines for tickets, except on the last four days.

✉ All England Lawn Tennis and Croquet Club, Church Road, SW19
☎ 020 8946 2244
🚇 Southfields

CRYSTAL PALACE NATIONAL SPORTS CENTRE

The major venue for national competitions.

✉ Ledrington Road SE19 ☎ 020 8778 0131 🚇 Crystal Palace

LORD'S CRICKET GROUND

Home of the MCC (Marylebone Cricket Club ► 62); watch Middlesex play home games, test cricket, major finals, and Sunday league games.

➕ D3 ✉ St. John's Wood Road, NW8 ☎ 020 7432 1066 🚇 St. John's Wood

THE OVAL

Surrey home games and test cricket; also Sunday league games.

➕ H8 ✉ Surrey County Cricket Club, The Oval, SE11 ☎ 020 7582 6660 🚇 Oval

ROYAL ALBERT HALL

Grand Victorian building holding 5,000 spectators; boxing, tennis, and sumo-wrestling events.

➕ C6 ✉ Kensington Gore, SW7 ☎ 020 7589 8212 🚇 South Kensington

OTHER MAJOR SPORTS

ASSOCIATION FOOTBALL (SOCCER)

Visit one of the 12 London clubs (Aug–May) such as Arsenal, Chelsea, Fulham, or Tottenham Hotspur.

AUTO RACING

Plenty of action at Brands Hatch in Kent: racing most weekends of the year, usually motorcycles on Saturdays, cars on Sundays.

HORSE RACING

A British obsession, so there are plenty of races near London during the flat season (Mar–Nov) and winter steeple-chasing (Aug–May). On and off course, betting is legal and well governed. Daytime races at Newmarket, Epsom, Goodwood, and Ascot can be reached by train from London, or take the train out to Windsor or Kempton for a delightful summer evening meeting. Daily newspapers have details of race meetings.

RUGBY UNION

Tickets for the internationals at Twickenham are scarce; it is easier to watch the Varsity match (Dec), the Cup Final (Apr–May), or take in a tour game, and easier still to watch a game at one of the ten London clubs such as Wasps or Harlequins.

You can watch and play most sports either in or near London (often merely an underground ride away). Major events are held on Saturdays and Sundays; tickets are readily available (see ticket agencies ► 80).

PARTICIPATORY SPORTS

London's many parks and open spaces are alive with people playing tennis, bowls, cricket and soccer, or jogging, walking, and boating. For more formal sports, Crystal Palace National Sports Centre has comprehensive facilities; but Kensington Sports Centre (✉ Walmer Road, W1), the Oasis (✉ 32 Endell Street, WC2), and the Queen Mother Sports Centre (✉ 223 Vauxhall Bridge Road, SW1) are more central. Barbican Health & Fitness Centre and Broadgate Club (at the Broadgate Centre, ► 56) have good fitness equipment.

85

Luxury Hotels

PRICES

Expect to pay the following prices per night for a single room, excluding V.A.T:

Luxury   more than £280
Mid-range   £100–£280
Budget   less than £100

BARGAIN DEALS

To be pampered amid sumptuous surroundings may be an essential part of your vacation. London's most luxurious hotels have been built with no expense spared. Although London hotel prices are generally very high, quality rooms can be had for bargain prices. It's always worth asking when you make your reservation whether any special deals are available. Most deluxe and mid-range hotels offer weekend deals throughout the year, often including breakfast, dinner, and sometimes theater tickets. The big chains such as Forte, Mount Charlotte Thistle, and Best Western have brochures offering package deals. Newly refurbished hotels usually have incentive prices, and off-season months such as January and February are a buyer's market.

CLARIDGE'S

From the art deco lobby and mirrored dining room to the huge baths and log fires in the corner suites, this is deluxe Mayfair living. 139 rooms.
⊞ E5 ✉ Brook Street, W1
☎ 020 7629 8860, fax 020 7499 2210 Ⓜ Bond Street

DORCHESTER

Deliciously art deco, a London landmark from its grand entrance and piano bar to its Oliver Messel suite. 250 rooms.
⊞ E6 ✉ Park Lane, W1
☎ 020 7629 8888, fax 020 7409 0114 Ⓜ Green Park, Hyde Park Corner

HALKIN HOTEL

Central London's first deluxe hotel built and furnished in contemporary design throughout, with a suitably upscale Italian restaurant. Ideal location for visits to Knightsbridge and Mayfair. 41 rooms.
⊞ E6 ✉ 4 Halkin Street, SW1 ☎ 020 7333 1000, fax 020 7333 1100 Ⓜ Hyde Park Corner

MANDARIN ORIENTAL HYDE PARK

New owners are injecting new life back into this grand hotel. With top-class service, you also get stunning views over Hyde Park. 200 rooms.
⊞ E6 ✉ Knightsbridge, SW1
☎ 020 7235 2000, fax 020 7235 4552 Ⓜ Knightsbridge

METROPOLITAN

Lush Hyde Park views contrast with uncompromisingly contemporary minimal interiors; high style bar. 155 rooms.

⊞ E6 ✉ Old Park Lane, W1
☎ 020 7447 10000, fax 020 7447 1147 Ⓜ Hyde Park Corner

ONE ALDWYCH

This stylish contemporary hotel fitted into an Edwardian building epitomizes London's current hotel fashion restrained luxury.
105 rooms.
⊞ G5 ✉ Aldwych, WC2
☎ 020 7300 1000, fax 020 7300 1101 Ⓜ Covent Garden or Temple

THE RITZ

Small but sumptuous, with plenty of old style, gilt decor, and the great first-floor promenade to London's most beautiful dining room, overlooking Green Park. 131 rooms.
⊞ F6 ✉ Piccadilly, W1
☎ 020 7493 8181, fax 020 7493 2687 Ⓜ Green Park

ST. MARTIN'S LANE

Theatrical minimalism at Ian Schrager and Philippe Starck's fabulously located hotel that opened in 1999; art, theater, opera, and restaurants are a mere step away. 204 rooms.
⊞ G5 ✉ St. Martin's Lane, WC2 ☎ 020 7300 5500, fax 020 7300 5501 Ⓜ Covent Garden or Leicester Square

SAVOY

Old-style Thameside hotel between the West End and the City; splendid river suites; art deco rooms; health club. 207 rooms.
⊞ G5 ✉ Strand, WC2
☎ 020 7836 4343, fax 020 7872 8901 Ⓜ Embankment

Mid-Range Hotels

ACADEMY

Excellent location for the British Museum set in four converted Georgian town houses with exceptionally light, modern rooms. 50 rooms.

➕ F4 ✉ 17–21 Gower Street, WC1 ☎ 020 7631 4115, fax 020 7636 3442 🚇 Goodge Street

BASIL STREET HOTEL

Tucked behind Harrods with old-style comforts, favored by discerning Americans. 8 rooms.

➕ D7 ✉ Basil Street, SW3 ☎ 020 7581 3311, fax 020 7581 3693 🚇 Knightsbridge

BLAKES

Sumptuous decadence achieved by designer Anoushka Hempel. 51 rooms.

➕ C8 ✉ 33 Roland Gardens, SW7 ☎ 020 7370 6701, fax 020 7373 0442 🚇 South Kensington

CHARLOTTE STREET HOTEL

Kit and Tim Kemp's boutique cocktail of serious comfort and fairytale Englishness. 3 other hotels in London. 52 rooms.

➕ F4 ✉ 15 Charlotte Street, W1 ☎ 020 7806 2000 , fax 020 7806 2002 🚇 Goodge Street

GORING

High standards of old-fashioned hospitality and service make this splendid hotel memorable. Owned by the Goring family for almost a century. 74 rooms.

➕ F7 ✉ Beeston Place, Grosvenor Gardens, SW1 ☎ 020 7396 9000, fax 020 7834 4393 🚇 Victoria

THE LEONARD

Discreet, stylish small hotel, near Oxford Street; comfortable, superbly decorated bedrooms. 31 rooms.

➕ D5 ✉ 15 Seymour Street, W1 ☎ 020 7935 2010, fax 020 7935 6700 🚇 Marble Arch

PORTOBELLO

Romantic retreat with exotic, sumptuous rooms, near the antiques shops of Portobello Road. 24 rooms.

➕ A5 ✉ 22 Stanley Gardens, W11 ☎ 020 7727 2777, fax 020 7792 9641 🚇 Notting Hill Gate

ROOKERY

Discreet comforts in this wonderfully atmospheric small hotel in Clerkenwell, with antiques, open fires, and Victorian bathrooms. 33 rooms.

➕ H4 ✉ 12 St. Peter's Lane, EC1 ☎ 020 7336 0931, fax 020 7336 0932 🚇 Farringdon

THE STAFFORD

Tucked behind Piccadilly, with an alley through to Green Park, this is a small, discreet hotel whose cozy, intimate public rooms are open to non-guests. 81 rooms.

➕ F6 ✉ 16 St. James's Place, SW1 ☎ 020 7493 0111, fax 020 7493 7121 🚇 Green Park

WESTBOURNE

Oriental modernism throughout, Japanese gardens, and rooms stocked with modern British art and DVD players. 20 rooms.

➕ B5 ✉ 163–5 Westbourne Grove ☎ 020 7243 6008, fax 020 7229 7201 🚇 Notting Hill Gate

BEWARE OF HIDDEN HOTEL COSTS

The room price quoted by a hotel may, or may not, include continental breakfast or full English breakfast and V.A.T., which is currently 17½ percent. Since these affect the final check dramatically, it is vital to ask in advance. Also, check the percentage mark-up on telephone calls, which can be high–there may even be charges for using a telephone charge card or receiving a fax; and ask about the laundry and pressing service, which can be very slow.

MODERN HOTELS

London has a plethora of contemporary hotels, from starkly minimal to sumptuously luxurious. At the top end, try the Metropolitan, One Aldwych, St. Martins's Lane (▶ 86), and the Hempel. Schrager and Startk's Sanderson, No. 5 Maddox Street, myhotel Bloomsbury, and the renovated Great Eastern Hotel in the mid-range.

Budget Accommodations

LOCATION IS EVERYTHING

It is well worth perusing the London map to decide where you are likely to spend most of your time. Then select a hotel in that area or accessible to it by underground on a direct line, so you avoid having to change trains. London is vast and it takes time to cross it, particularly by bus and costly taxis. By paying a little more to be in the center and near your activities, you will save on travel time and costs.

BED & BREAKFAST

Stay in a carefully chosen private house in London for both the venue and the friendliness of the hosts. Prices to suit all budgets.

London Bed and Breakfast Agency
✉ 71 Fellows Road, NW3 3JY
☎ 020 7586 2768, fax 020 7586 6567, www.londonbb.com

YOUTH HOSTELS

There are seven hostels in central London (by Oxford Street, in Holland Park, and by St. Paul's Cathedral, for example), so be sure to reserve well ahead.

Youth Hostels Association
✉ Trevelyan House, 8 St. Stephen's Hill, St. Albans, Hertfordshire, AL1 2DY
☎ 01727 855215, fax 01727 844126. Reservations 020 7373 3400, fax 020 7236 7681

5 SUMNER PLACE HOTEL

Family-run house-hotel, in a South Kensington area; conservatory and a garden. 13 rooms.
➕ C7 ✉ 5 Sumner Place, SW7 ☎ 020 7584 7586, fax 020 7823 9962 Ⓣ South Kensington

EURO HOTEL

Stylish Bloomsbury setting for a small, charming bed and breakfast. 35 rooms.
➕ G4 ✉ 51–3 Cartwright Gardens, Russell Square, WC1 ☎ 020 7387 4321, fax 020 7383 5044 Ⓣ Russell Square

GENERATOR

This stylish, industrial-style building offers 800 guests bunk-bedded rooms but excellent facilities. 217 rooms. (internet, canteen, and bar).
➕ G4 ✉ Compton Place, Tavistock Place, WC1 ☎ 020 7388 7666, fax 020 7388 7644 Ⓣ Russell Square

INTERNATIONAL STUDENTS HOUSE

Rooms and family flats right by Regent's Park. Reserve well ahead. 158 rooms.
➕ F4 ✉ 229 Great Portland Street, W1 ☎ 020 7631 8300, fax 020 7631 8315 Ⓣ Great Portland Street or Regent's Park

KENSINGTON MANOR HOTEL

Well-placed for South Kensington museums and Knightsbridge shopping. 14 rooms.
➕ C7 ✉ 8 Emperors Gate, SW7 ☎ 020 7370 7516, fax 020 7373 3163 Ⓣ Gloucester Road

LONDON HOMESTEAD SERVICES

Try this agency if you want to stay with a London family: 200 homes within 20 minutes of Piccadilly. Minimum three-night stay.
✉ Coombe Wood Road, Kingston-upon-Thames, Surrey ☎ 020 8949 4455, fax 020 8549 5492

SWISS HOUSE HOTEL

Comfortable little hotel in a pretty residential area of South Kensington. 15 rooms.
➕ C8 ✉ 171 Old Brompton Road, SW5 ☎ 020 7373 2769, fax 020 7373 4983 Ⓣ Earl's Court or Gloucester Road

UNIVERSITY WOMEN'S CLUB

Located in an old Mayfair house; membership open to all women graduates and similarly qualified women; friends pay a temporary membership fee. 24 rooms.
➕ E6 ✉ 2 Audley Square, South Audley Street, W1 ☎ 020 7499 2268, fax 020 7499 7046 Ⓣ Hyde Park Corner

TRAVEL INN

Practical, dependable, no frills chain whose star London location is in County Hall, opposite the Houses of Parliament. 313 rooms.
➕ G6 ✉ County Hall, Belvedere Road, SE1 ☎ 020 7902 1600, fax 020 7902 1619 Ⓣ Waterloo

VICTORIA INN

Friendly, stucco-fronted Pimlico house with no-frills. 43 rooms.
➕ F7 ✉ 65–7 Belgrave Road, SW1 ☎ 020 7834 6721, fax 020 7931 0201 Ⓣ Victoria

LONDON
travel facts

UNDERGROUND

ESSENTIAL FACTS

Britain information

- Britain Visitor Centre ✉ 1 Regent Street, south of Piccadilly Circus, SW1 ☎ website: www.visitbritain.com ⏰ Mon–Fri 9–6:30; Sat–Sun 10–4. Jun–Oct: Sat 9–5
- British Tourist Authority information service ☎ 020 8846 9000

Tourist information centers

- London Tourist Board centers: ☎ website: www.londontown.com
- ✉ Victoria station forecourt, SW1 ⏰ Daily The largest center, with comprehensive London information and hotel booking service. Free maps for roads, buses, and subway (underground), plus events sheets.
- ✉ Heathrow Terminals 1, 2, and 3 underground station, Heathrow Airport ⏰ Daily
- ✉ Liverpool Street underground station, EC2 ⏰ Daily
- ✉ Waterloo International Terminus, SE1 ⏰ Daily

Local centers

- For detailed information on the City of London: City of London Information Centre ✉ St. Paul's Churchyard, EC4 ☎ 020 7332 1456 ⏰ Daily 9:30–5. Oct–Mar: closed Sun
- Greenwich Tourist Information Centre ✉ 2 Cutty Sark Gardens, Greenwich, SE10 ☎ 0870 608 2000 ⏰ Daily
- Richmond Tourist Information Centre ✉ Old Town Hall, Whittaker Avenue, Richmond, Surrey ☎ 020 8940 9125 ⏰ Mon–Sat; Sun in summer
- Southwark Tourist Information Centre ✉ 6 Tooley Street, SE1 ☎ 020 7403 8299 ⏰ Daily

Hotel reservations

- The London Tourist Board ☎ 020 7932 2020 publishes an annual hotel guide, *Where to Stay in London*, and runs a hotel booking service; credit card payment only. £5 fee.
- The Automobile Association (AA) publishes an annual hotel guide (available from bookstores), *The Hotel Guide*, covering the whole of Britain with a section on London. Their hotel booking service ☎ 0870 5050505 is free for its members but a database of all AA inspected hotels can be found on their website. To find out more about the AA, visit them on: www.theaa.co.uk.

London Line

- 24-hour recorded telephone guide ☎ 09068 063344 covering a wide range of subjects. Premium rates are charged. To access specific information, constantly updated, dial the number and then follow the instructions. Subjects to choose from vary from London attractions and riverboat trips to theater, children's events, shopping, and eating out.
- Other useful information numbers: Tower bridge opening: ☎ 020 7378 7700; for football information: ☎ 0930 555888. To book rock and pop concerts, London shows, and big events, call Ticketmaster ☎ 020 7344 4444 or Firstcall ☎ 020 7420 1000

Electricity

- Standard supply is 240V.
- Motor-driven equipment needs a specific frequency; in the U.K. it is 50 cycles per second (kHz).

Opening hours

- Major attractions: seven days a week; some open late on Sun.
- Stores: six days a week; some open on Sun. For late-night shopping (► 72).
- Banks: Mon–Fri 9:30–5; a few remain open later or open on Sat

mornings. Bureaux de change have longer opening hours (including weekends).

- Post offices: usually Mon–Fri 9–5:30; Sat 9–12:30.

Places of worship

- Almost every denomination is represented. Refer to the Yellow Pages telephone directory.

Public holidays

- Jan 1; Good Friday; Easter Mon; May Day (first Mon in May); last Mon in May; last Mon in Aug; Dec 25; Dec 26.
- Almost all attractions and stores close Christmas Day; many close Dec 24, Jan 1, and Good Fri as well. Stores, restaurants, and attractions remain open on other holidays but it is advisable to check in advance.

Tipping

- 10 percent for restaurants, taxis, hairdressers, and other services. Look over restaurant checks to see if service charge has already been added or is included.
- No tipping in theaters, movies, concert halls, or in pubs and bars (unless there is waitress service).

PUBLIC TRANSPORTATION

London Transport travel information centers

- Centers sell travel passes and provide underground and train maps, bus route maps, and information on cheap tickets.
- 🕔 Daily at each terminal at Heathrow Airport and at the following stations: 🚇 Hammersmith, Oxford Circus (except Sun), Piccadilly Circus, St. James's Park (except Sun), and Heathrow Terminals 1, 2, and 3 🚆 Victoria, Euston, King's Cross, Paddington
- London Transport inquiries

telephone service ☎ 020 7222 1234 (🕔 24 hours); 020 7222 1200.

Travel Passes

- Travelcards: valid after 9:30AM for unlimited travel by underground, railroad, Docklands Light Railway, and most buses; sold at travel information centers, British Rail stations, all underground stations, and some stores, cover travel for one day, a week, a weekend, a month, or a year. Adults need a photocard (except for a one-day travelcard), sold at travel information centers; children aged 5–15 pay child fares but need a child-rate photocard; children under five travel free.
- Bus passes: bus-only passes are on sale at travel information centers, underground stations, and some newsdealers.
- Visitor travelcards: similar to travelcards but no need for a photo; valid for one, three, four, or seven days. Must be bought before arrival in London.
- Carnet: a book of 10 tickets for Zone 1 only.

The underground (the tube)

- Twelve color-coded lines link almost 300 stations. Use a travel pass or buy a ticket from a machine (some give change) or ticket booth; keep the ticket until the end of the journey. The system includes the Docklands Light Railway (DLR) and the Jubilee line extension, opened in 1999.

Buses

- Plan your journey using the latest copy of the *All London Bus Guide*, available at tourist offices .
- A bus stop is indicated by a red sign on a metal pole.
- On a two-man bus, the conductor

comes to inspect the travel pass or sell a ticket; on a one-man bus, the driver inspects passes or sells tickets as passengers board—try to have the exact change.

Taxis

- Drivers of official (mostly black) cabs know the city well. They are obliged to follow the shortest route unless an alternative is agreed. A black cab is licensed for up to five passengers.
- Meter charges increase in the evenings and on weekends.
- Avoid minicabs; they may have no meter and inadequate insurance.
- Black cabs can be ordered by phone: Computer Cab ☎ 020 7286 0286; Radio Taxis ☎ 020 7272 0272

MEDIA & COMMUNICATIONS

Newspapers & magazines

- Quality papers include *The Times*, the *Financial Times*, the *Daily Telegraph*, the *Independent*, the *Guardian*, and the *Sunday Times*, *Sunday Telegraph*, *Observer*, and *Independent on Sunday*.
- London's only evening paper, the *Evening Standard* (Mon–Fri), first edition out around noon, is strong on entertainment and nightlife.
- *Time Out* (published weekly on Wednesdays) lists almost everything going.

Sending a letter or a postcard

- Stamps are sold at post offices and some newsstands and stores.
- Trafalgar Square Post Office stays open till late: ✉ William IV Street, WC2 🕐 Mon–Sat 8–8
- Mailboxes are red.

Telephones

- Check the mark-up rate before making a call from a hotel.

- London numbers (now 8 digits) are prefixed with the code 020 when dialing from outside the city.
- Use coins or a British Telecom (BT) phonecard to call from BT phone booths. Phonecards are sold at post offices and newsstands. Many phones take credit cards.
- Information ☎ 192
- Operator ☎ 100 to check costs, call collect, or call another person in the U.K. via the operator.
- International telephoning: ☎ 153 for directory inquiries; ☎ 155 to call collect.
- Beware of high charges on some premium rate numbers (prefixed 09) and special rate (08) numbers.

Television

- BBC 1 (varied); BBC 2 (more cultural); ITV (commercial— varied); Channel 4 (commercial— cultural and minority interest); Channel 5 (commercial—varied); satellite and cable channels (mainly in larger hotels) include CNN, MTV, and Sky. A few provide digital T.V.

EMERGENCIES

Emergency telephone numbers

- For police, fire, or ambulance, ☎ 999 from any telephone, free of charge. The call goes directly to the emergency services. Tell the operator which street you are on and the nearest landmark, intersection, or house number; stay by the telephone until help arrives.

Embassies & missions

- Australian High Commission ✉ Australia House, Strand, WC2 ☎ 020 7379 4334
- Canadian High Commission ✉ 38 Grosvenor Street, W1 ☎ 020 7258 6600
- Irish Embassy ✉ 17 Grosvenor Place,

SW1 ☎ 020 7235 2171
- New Zealand High Commission
  ✉ New Zealand House, 80 Haymarket, SW1
  ☎ 020 7930 8422
- Embassy of the United States of
  America ✉ 24 Grosvenor Square, W1
  ☎ 020 7499 9000

Lost credit cards
- Report any loss immediately to the
  relevant company and to the
  nearest police station; also call your
  bank.
- To discover your credit card
  company's local 24-hour
  emergency number ☎ 192
  (information).

Medical treatment
- E.U. nationals and citizens of
  some other countries with special
  arrangements (Australia and New
  Zealand) may receive free
  National Health Service (NHS)
  medical treatment. Others pay.
- If you need an ambulance ☎ 999
  on any telephone, free of charge.
- NHS hospitals with 24-hour
  emergency departments include:
  University College Hospital
  ✉ Gower Street (entrance in Grafton Way), WC1
  ☎ 020 7387 9300; Chelsea and
  Westminster Hospital ✉ 369 Fulham
  Road, SW10 ☎ 020 8746 8000
- Private hospitals, with no
  emergency unit, include the
  Cromwell Hospital ✉ Cromwell Road,
  SW5 ☎ 020 7460 2000
- Great Chapel Street Medical
  Centre ✉ 13 Great Chapel Street, W1
  ☎ 020 7437 9360 is an NHS clinic
  open to all, but visitors from
  countries without the NHS
  reciprocal agreement must pay.
- Dental specialist: contact British
  Dental Association ☎ 020 7935 0875.
  Helpline 0870 3331188
- Eye specialist: Moorfields Eye
  Hospital ✉ City Road, EC1 ☎ 020 7253

3411; Dolland & Aitchison
✉ 229–31 Regent Street, W1 ☎ 020 7499
8777 (opticians and on-site
workshop for glasses and contact
lenses).
- For homeopathic pharmacies,
  practitioners, and advice: the
  British Homeopathic Association
  ✉ 27a Devonshire Street, W1 ☎ 020 7566
  7800

Medicines
- Many drugs cannot be bought
  over the counter. For an NHS
  prescription, pay a modest flat
  rate; if a private doctor prescribes,
  you pay the full cost. To claim
  charges back on insurance, keep
  receipts.
- Drugstores open late include:
  Bliss Chemist ✉ 5 Marble Arch, W1
  ☎ 020 7723 6116 🕐 Daily 9AM–midnight
- Ainsworth's Homeopathic
  Pharmacy ✉ 38 New Cavendish Street
  ☎ 020 7935 5330 🕐 Mon–Fri 9–5:30;
  Sat 9–4.

Sensible precautions
- Do not wear valuables that can be
  snatched. If you must bring
  valuables, put them in a hotel or
  bank safe box.
- Make a note of all passport, ticket,
  and credit card numbers, and
  keep it in a separate place.
- Keep money, passport, and credit
  cards in a fully closed bag. Carry
  only a small amount of cash and
  keep it out of sight.
- Keep your bag in sight at all
  times—do not sling it over your
  back or put it on the floor of a
  café, pub, or movie theater. Keep
  an eye on all other shopping bags.
- At night, try not to travel alone; if
  you must, either pre-book a taxi or
  keep to well-lit streets and use a
  bus or underground train where
  there are already other people.

Index

Citypack
London

AUTHOR AND EDITION REVISER *Louise Nicholson*
CONTRIBUTIONS TO LIVING LONDON *Paul Wade and Kathy Arnold*
MANAGING EDITOR *Hilary Weston*
COVER DESIGN *Tigist Getachew, Fabrizio La Rocca*

Copyright   © 1996, 1997, 1999, 2002 by The Automobile Association
Maps Copyright   © 1996, 1999, 2002 by The Automobile Association
Fold-out map   © Mairs Geographischer Verlag, Germany

ISBN 0–676–90166–2

FOURTH EDITION

ACKNOWLEDGMENTS
The Automobile Association would like to thank the following photographers, libraries, and associations for their assistance in the preparation of this book.
BRIDGEMAN ART LRRARY, LONDON 16l The Tower of London, from a survey made in 1597 by W. Haiward and J Gascoyne (engraving) by English School (19th century) Stapleton Collection, UK, 16/17 Great Fire of London, 1666 by Lieve Verschuier (1630-86) Museum of Fine Arts, Budapest, Hungary; BRITISH MUSEUM 45; HULTON GETTY 17l, 17r; NATIONAL PORTRAIT GALLERY 40t, 40b; PICTOR INTERNATIONAL, LONDON 24r; ROBERT HARDING PICTURE LIBRARY 14l, 14c, 19l, 24l, 60; SCIENCE MUSEUM 29; SPECTRUM COLOUR LIBRARY 31, 34; STOCKBYTE 5.
The remaining photographs are held in the Association's own library (AA PHOTO LIBRARY) and were taken by MAX JOURDAN with the exception of the following:
PETER BAKER cover: Tower Bridge; CAROLINE JONES 21; PAUL KENWARD 20tc, 22tr; S & O MATHEWS cover: St Paul's Cathedral; 48b; JENNY MCMILLAN 24tr; JOHN MILLER 7; ROBERT MORT cover: telephone box, 20r, 50b, 56; BARRIE SMITH cover: Westminster Abbey, man at antique market, 26t, 26b, 27, 32b, 37t, 42t; RICK STRANGE cover: Underground sign, Royal Albert Hall, 21tc, 28t, 28b, 30t, 30b, 32t, 33, 48t, 49, 51t, 52, 62; JAMES A TIMS cover: taxi, 23tl; MARTIN TRELAWNY 21tl, 23tc, 44t, 58; ROY VICTOR cover: guard, 25t; PETER WILSON 41, 46b, 55; TIM WOODCOCK 35t, 36, 39b, 46t, 57; WYN VOYSEY 6tr, 35b, 37b, 38, 42b, 50t, 59.

IMPORTANT NOTE
Time inevitably brings changes, so always confirm prices, travel facts, and other perishable information when it matters. Although Fodor's cannot accept responsibility for errors, you can use this guide in the confidence that we have taken every care to ensure its accuracy.

SPECIAL SALES
Fodor's Travel Publications are available at special discounts for bulk purchases (100 copies or more) for sales promotions or premiums. Special editions, including personalized covers, excerpts of existing guides, and corporate imprints, can be created in large quantities for special needs. For more information, contact your local bookseller or write to Special Markets, Fodor's Travel Publications, 201 East 50th Street, New York, NY 10022. Inquiries from Canada should be directed to your local Canadian bookseller or sent to Random House of Canada, Ltd., Marketing Department, 2775 Matheson Boulevard East, Mississauga, Ontario L4W 4P7.

Color separation by Daylight Colour Art Pte Ltd, Singapore
Manufactured by Dai Nippon Printing Co. (Hong Kong) Ltd
10 9 8 7 6 5 4 3 2 1

TITLES IN THE CITYPACK SERIES
• Amsterdam • Bangkok • Barcelona • Beijing • Berlin • Boston •
• Brussels & Bruges • Chicago • Dublin • Florence • Hong Kong • Lisbon •
• London • Los Angeles • Madrid • Melbourne • Miami • Montreal • Munich •
• New York City • Paris • Prague • Rome • San Francisco • Seattle • Shanghai •
• Singapore • Sydney • Tokyo • Toronto • Venice • Vienna • Washington D. C. •